Anonymous

Report Presented at the Annual Meeting of the Sixteenth Anniversary

of the New South Wales Institution for the Deaf and Dumb and...

Anonymous

Report Presented at the Annual Meeting of the Sixteenth Anniversary
of the New South Wales Institution for the Deaf and Dumb and...

ISBN/EAN: 9783744763240

Printed in Europe, USA, Canada, Australia, Japan

Cover: Foto ©ninafisch / pixelio.de

More available books at **www.hansebooks.com**

REPORT

PRESENTED AT THE

ANNUAL MEETING OF THE SIXTEENTH ANNIVERSARY

OF THE

New South Wales Institution

FOR THE

DEAF AND DUMB AND THE BLIND,

For the Year Ending 30th September, 1877,

WITH

THE TREASURER'S BALANCE SHEETS,

LISTS OF DONATIONS AND SUBSCRIPTIONS,

AND

Information Concerning the Admission of Children.

Sydney :

JOSEPH COOK & CO., PRINTERS, 370, GEORGE-STREET.

OPPOSITE THE BANK OF NEW SOUTH WALES.

1877.

OFFICE BEARERS AND COMMITTEE
For the year ending 30th September, 1878.

Patron:
HIS EXCELLENCY SIR HERCULES ROBINSON, K.C.B., &c.

President:
THE REV. GEORGE KING, M.A.

Vice-President:
THE REV. DR. LANG.

Hon. Treasurer:
HENRY PHILLIPS, ESQ.

Hon. Secretary:
ELLIS ROBINSON, ESQ.,
486, *George-street, Sydney.*

Hon. Surgeon:
ARTHUR RENWICK, ESQ., M.D.

Committee:

E. T. BEILBY, ESQ.
S. C. BROWN, ESQ. M.L.A.
JOHN FRAZER, The Hon., M.L.C.
J. R. FAIRFAX, ESQ.
ROBERT HILLS, ESQ.
JAMES HENRY, ESQ.
J. R. LINSLEY, ESQ., J.P.

J. R. LOVE, ESQ.
REV. JAMES MILNE, M.A.
JOHN MILLS, ESQ.
JOSEPH PAXTON, ESQ. J.P.
F. R. ROBINSON, ESQ.
E. SABER, ESQ.
REV. WILLIAM SCOTT, M.A.

GEORGE F. WISE, ESQ.

Ladies' Visiting Committee:

MRS. BAILLIE,
MRS. BREILLAT,
MRS. J. H. GOODLET,
MRS. JOHN HAY,
MRS. THOMAS HOLT,
MRS. GEORGE KING,

MRS. J. R. LOVE,
MISS MACKIE,
MRS. J. PAXTON,
MRS. H. PHILLIPS,
MRS. F. R. ROBINSON,
MRS. W. SCOTT.

Master:
MR. SAMUEL WATSON.

Matron: | **Matron's Assistant:**
MRS. ASHTON. | MISS CAMPBELL.

Music Teacher and Instructor of the Blind:
MISS C. SHARP, L.A.M.

Clerk and Collector:
MR. GEORGE LUFF.

Pupil Teacher:
MISS CHRISTINA CAMERON.

The Institution is open to Subscribers and other Visitors daily, from 2 until 4 o'clock p.m., Saturdays, Sundays, and Holidays excepted.

LIFE DIRECTORS.

APPOINTED UNDER RULE IV·

Clause 3.

KING, REV. GEORGE, M.A. | ROBINSON, F. R. ESQ.
LOVE, WILLIAM, ESQ., J.P.

Clause 4.

ROBINSON, ELLIS, ESQ. | PHILLIPS, H. ESQ.

Clause 5.

LANG, REV. DR. | FRAZER, JOHN, ESQ., J.P.

Clause 6.

BELMORE, His Excellency The Right Hon. Earl of
PAXTON, JOSEPH, ESQ. | WALKER, THOMAS, ESQ.,
HOLTERMANN, B. O. ESQ. | CAMPBELL, W. B. ESQ.

Clause 7.

JOY, EDWARD, ESQ. | WISE, GEORGE F., ESQ.

Names of Donors of £50 and upwards in aid of the Funds of the Institution.

His Excellency the Right Hon. Earl of Belmore. Donations £350.

Fairfax and Sons. ...Donation £100	William Manson ... Bequest £1000	
Mrs. Mary Roberts ,, 100	William Keel ... ,, 150	
James Williams ... Bequest 100	John W. Wood ...Donation 100	
Maurice Alexander ,, 50	B. O. Holtermann ,, 100	
Dr. Charles Muller ... Don. 100	Joseph Paxton, J.P. ,, 50	
Hon. John Frazer... ... ,, 50	Hamilton Hume ... Bequest 50	
Bryan Fall ... ... Bequest 50	William Moffitt ... ,, 250	
Thomas Walker ... Donation 200	Hugh Nolan ... ... ,, 100	
John W. Wood ... Bequest 1000	Thomas Frost... ... ,, 100	
Mrs. Sarah White ,, 50	Button Charles ... ,, 50	

RESOLUTIONS passed at the Sixteenth Annual Meeting, held at the INSTITUTION, Newtown Road, on MONDAY AFTERNOON, 8th October, 1877.

HIS EXCELLENCY SIR HERCULES ROBINSON, K.C.B., &c., in the Chair.

Moved by the REV. GEORGE KING,
Seconded by M. LEVY, ESQ., J.P. :—

"That the Report now read be adopted, and, together with the balance-sheet be printed for circulation." Carried unanimously.

Moved by the REV. DR. LANG,
Seconded by the REV. W. SCOTT :—

"That the thanks of this Meeting are hereby given to the Government and Parliament for the annual donation of £450, in aid of the funds of the Institution."—Carried unanimously.

Moved by the REV. S. WILKINSON,
Seconded by the REV. H. MACREADIE :—

"That the following gentlemen do constitute the Committee for the ensuing year :—*President*, the Rev. George King, M.A.; *Vice-President*, Rev. Dr. Lang ; *Hon. Treasurer*, Mr. Henry Phillips : *Hon. Secretary*, Mr. Ellis Robinson ; *Hon. Surgeon*, Mr. Arthur Renwick, M.D.; *Committee*, Mr. E. T. Beilby, Mr. S. C. Brown, M.L.A., Hon. John Frazer, M.L.C., Mr. J. R. Fairfax, Mr. Robert Hills, Mr. James Henry, Mr. J. R. Linsley, J.P., Rev. James Milne, M.A., Mr. F. R. Robinson, Mr. George F. Wise, Mr. J. R. Love, Mr. Joseph Paxton, Mr. E. Saber, Mr. John Mills, Rev. Wm. Scott."

SIXTEENTH ANNUAL REPORT

OF THE

NEW SOUTH WALES

Institution for the Deaf & Dumb, & the Blind,

For the year ending September 30th, 1877.

The Committee have very great pleasure in submitting for the information and approval of the Subscribers and Friends, their Sixteenth Annual Report of the position and proceedings of the Institution for the past twelve months—and in congratulating all interested in the progress made. The first subject meriting attention—

THE PROGRESS OF THE PUPILS.

Is as usual quite satisfactory, those pupils who have left during the year have in all cases proved to their friends the substantial character and basis on which the Education imparted at the Institution is founded. Even the dullest and most stupid intellects have profited by the instruction. *New Books*—The Australian Edition for the use of Public Schools has been adopted (2 or 3 months ago) as far as the peculiar necessities of the Inmates would permit, a shipment of Books for both the Deaf and Dumb, and the Blind is daily expected from England, and a fresh supply of maps has been obtained.

The instruction in music to the Blind and in drawing to the Deaf and Dumb still continues, Mr. Watson has a few of the most forward of the elder Boys of the latter class under instruction in Rudiments of French.

The Annual Examination was held in December last and passed off satisfactorily, prizes were awarded to the most proficient.

Health of the Pupils.

Has been more than usually good, no sickness of any moment having to be recorded during the year. The Hospital apartments having been almost wholly unoccupied. Dr. Renwick's gratuitous services again entitle him to the warmest thanks and most earnest good wishes of the Committee.

Number of Inmates.

At last Report there were 69 Inmates and 11 have been received since and 1 re-admitted, making a total of 81—11 have left, all of them having received a sufficient amount of Education to enable them to make their way in the world ; among those who have left—1 boy has gone to earn his living at chair caning, two girls apprenticed to Dress Making Establishments, 1 Blind girl returned to her friends, 1 boy is employed in Survey Department by Queensland Government, and 1 returned to New Zealand. There are several of the elder ones who will at the end of this year return to their friends to pursue their various paths in life, owing to this Institution an enormous debt for the knowledge they now have, to help them in obtaining their own livelihood and making them we hope useful and worthy members of the community.

Two of the children in Queensland were visited by one of the Directors while on a visit and were highly spoken of by all who came in contact with them.

Financial.

The amount of Subscriptions and Donations has increased £100 0s. 3d. Those from the country still continue very satisfactory and the Committee would beg here to thank many kind friends who have taken lists and collected during this year, and in many ways helped to augment the funds.

The number of Inmates has been greater and expenses have not lessened, all articles having to be purchased at a higher rate.

Special receipts and donations have to be noted as under— Legacy from Executors of late Charles Button, £50 ; also from Hon. James White, M.L.C., Executor of late Mrs. Sarah White, Legacy of £50.

Early in the year the Committee found it necessary to provide a buggy for the better carrying out of the country collecting by Mr. Luff, this has proved a great success.

The Committee notice with regret the very few Legacies or Bequests made to this Institution and would fondly hope some of the great wealth of the colony will be used in helping and providing for such worthy objects as the maintenance of so valuable and necessary an Institution as this. Mr. W. B. Campbell's charitable scheme of the " Golden Barrell " realized for the funds of the Institution the handsome sum of £100 10s. 11d., and the Committee in recognition of his valuable services have elected him a Life Director in accordance with the Rules.

The receipts for School Fees and Clothing show a marked increase this year and in a another portion of this Report special attention is drawn to this fact.

Improvements and Additions.

During the year the Committee applied for and obtained from the Mayor (B. Palmer, Esq.) and the Aldermen, permission to have a supply of the city water gratuitously and pipes have been laid on to the grounds, giving an additional source of supply above the ordinary supply. The laying on of this water was carried out by a member of the Committee at cost price, and the pipes of a size sufficiently large to be of use in case of fire alarm. Porches and seats have been erected in back verandahs.

Plans were prepared in January last and tenders called for the erection of the dwarf stone wall and piers for gates and railings of a plain substantial construction and design, the wall is completed and paid for, and a tender was accepted in July last for the railings and gates ; they will be completed in a few weeks, and the Committee hope to have funds enough to pay for all these improvements, and with the assistance of the friends carry out other improvements, viz. :—Fencing and Gates to the Garden &c., an ornamental play shed for the children during the heat of Summer, as well as some other.

The Numbers for the School and Dining Room having become too large, the Committee removed the School to one of the large rooms in the Boys' wing which gives more space to carry on the teaching operations.

GENERAL.

Another important matter the Committee desire to press urgently on the public and friends of the Institution, is the desirability in all cases of inducing the parents of these afflicted children to send them to the Institution early. Numerous cases have come before the Committee where they have good reason to presume that the neglect to send these children to be educated, has almost of a certainty resulted in their lapsing into a state of half Idocy from the want of the discipline and educational advantages to be obtained in this Institution. Some instances have happened this year where the children are now, or about to become inmates of an Asylum for Imbeciles.

The Committee have also to deeply regret the loss of the kind services of one of their Lady visitors through the death of Mrs. J. M. Dunsmure.

During the whole of this year the Committee have given their most earnest attention to the matter of School Fees and in many instances, after due enquiry, where the parents could afford it, have insisted on a higher rate of payment, resulting in an increased amount of Fees to the sum of £563 19s., as against £455 18s. 9d. last year, an increase of £108 1s.

The Committee desire to record their thanks and hearty appreciation of the kindness of several of the Steam Boat Companies in carrying at considerably reduced rates and in some cases free of charge the children to and from their homes during the year, thus giving many pupils a trip home who otherwise would not have it, to the great benefit of their health and also pecuniarily to the Funds of the Institution. And also to the Sydney United Omnibus Company for free 'busses on several occasions for the children. As also free admission to the Agricultural Society's Exhibition and the kind attention of Mr. Wallis and Mr. Joubert.

The Committee have again to acknowledge the very great kindness and attention shown on every side to the pupils and officers of the Institution while on their visits to various places, kind friends in all cases vieing with each other in their efforts to please and entertain the children; so numerous indeed are these instances as to render it almost impossible to enumerate them, but in the Report will be given a list of these friends.

The following very valuable and opportune services during the year are thankfully acknowledged. Mr. Wigzell, monthly to cut the children's hair; Mr. James Henry, Dentistry; picnics to the children by Mrs. John Hay, Mr. Elouis, Mrs. T. Holt; Mr. Richard Seymour's frequent donations of fresh fish; Colonial Sugar Company, donations of casks of treacle; the Civil Service Musical Society, free admission of the elder blind music pupils to their concerts; and many others, of which a detailed list will be printed with the report. There are also several ladies whose constant attendance to instruct the children in special subjects, and to read to the Blind pupils, are deserving of the warmest recognition.

The Committee also are indebted for the following newspapers, *Sydney Mail, Australian Churchman* and *Illustrated Sydney News.*

The Ladies' Visiting Committee still continue their good offices for the welfare of the children and all concerned, and exercise a wise discretion over the domestic concerns of the Establishment.

CONCLUSION.

In concluding the Committee sincerely commend the Institution and its afflicted inmates to the care of the Almighty Father, who for His own farseeing ends has sent amongst us these afflicted creatures and to Him the Committee desire to offer their heartfelt thanks for the success attending their efforts. The Committee desire to record the harmonious working together of all concerned, for the good effects and results of their arduous and continued exertions.

VISIT OF ROYAL COMMISSIONERS ON CHARITABLE INSTITUTIONS.

The gentlemen appointed as a Royal Commission to report upon the charities of the colony, paid a visit of inspection in due course to this Institution, and in their most exhaustive and able report notified their impressions as being most satisfactory, and the following extract from the Second Report of the Commissioners appointed to inquire into, and report upon, the Working aud Management of the Public Charities of the Colony, 29th May, 1874, page 117:—

"The Institution for the Deaf and Dumb and the Blind.—This Institution being to a small extent assisted by a Parliamentary vote, we made an inquiry into its management. We found it contained Twenty-one Deaf and Dumb Boys, and an equal number of Girls of the same class, besides Five Blind Boys and Seven Blind Girls, 54 in all. The management appeared to us to be good, and we remarked nothing calling for particular notice. The Institution is conducted on unsectarian principles, and from its truly charitable character, is in every way deserving of public support."

THE FOLLOWING NOTE OF THE DAY IN THE *Echo* OF OCT. 9TH IS PRINTED FOR THE INFORMATION OF SUBSCRIBERS.

"Among the public charities of New South Wales there does not appear to bo one which is prosecuting its work more successfully and pleasantly than the Institution for the Deaf and Dumb and the Blind. About seventy afflicted children have been under instruction during the past year, and the educational progress made by them seems to be entirely satisfactory. There is evidently no immediate danger of the institution being wrecked on the rock of finance. The income last year reached an aggregate of £2,860, of which amount the Government grant was only £450. It is gratifying to find that the public have responded so heartily to an appeal for these little ones who have been so heavily handicapped by Nature. Perhaps one reason why this institution is enabled to present so cheering a report is that it has never been associated with sectarian bickerings, or bitter jealousies, or unhappy misunderstandings. It has been chiefly managed by ladies, and perhaps we are justified in attributing to that fact the peace and harmony which have prevailed. It is a great pity that any public charity should be converted into a battle-ground. We are glad to learn that the committee have given their most earnest attention to the matter of fees, and have insisted on higher payments where parents are rich enough to afford them. There has been a suspicion abroad that some such action as this was necessary. The public are willing enough to assist poor people to get their deaf and dumb and blind children educated ; but the opulent need no such help. Tho Rev. George King, in moving the adoption of the report yesterday, said that those charitably disposed people who feared imposition might contribute to this institution with every feeling of confidence that their money will not be misdirected. This is true; and we trust those who have cash balances and generous hearts will take Mr. King's hint for the coming year."

The Following is the Report Presented to the Government and Parliament by the Inspector of Charities.

The Inspector of Charities reports of this Institution as follows :—

" This very popular and truly charitable institution is subsidized by Government only to the extent of £450, and is under the control of its own elected board and directory.

The objects set forth in its prospectus are to educate and maintain children deaf and dumb or blind, to enable them to earn their own living, make them useful members of society, and prevent them becoming burdensome to others in after life.

In order to enlarge the sphere of its operations, render the internal administration more economical, and so increase its means for imparting a thoroughly good system of education, the directors decided on admitting on certain conditions into the institution children from the neighbouring colonies of Queensland, Tasmania, and New Zealand, where to the present time no institutions of similar character exist. Among these conditions are two, viz. :—

1st. That a guarantee be given that a child on leaving the institution shall be conveyed to its own colony.

2nd. That its cost while in the school shall be paid by responsible parties to the extent of £25 per annum.

When obtainable, the above sum of £25 is always demanded, but pauper children residing in this colony are received free, and in cases where the parents or guardians cannot command the full sum, less is accepted after due inquiry.

No child is eligible under seven years of age, nor excepting in special cases, beyond twelve years.

As education can only be received slowly, owing to physical disability, pupils may continue in the institution until the age of eighteen. In the great majority of cases, however, they leave much earlier—say at fifteen or sixteen years old.

No trades are taught, experience in similar institutions elsewhere tending to show that it is preferable to confine the attention of pupils to their mental cultivation, leaving handicrafts to be acquired afterwards as apprentices, in ordinary workshops. I have not myself collected sufficient evidence to express any opinion as to the correctness of this theory, but in practical working the plan is unavoidable so long as the numbers to be taught are very limited, as at present is the case.

The domestic work of the establishment is all done by the pupils (the deaf mutes). The blind who show talent are taught music, with a view to its becoming a means of livelihood.

The conduct of such an institution has of course to be peculiar, and is in some respects necessarily expensive. The management appears excellent, and has the advantage of a ladies' committee, which works harmoniously with the matron of the institution. The children look clean and well cared for, happy and contented. As may be expected both from the slowness of its inception and the wide difference in the ages at which the pupils severally begin their education, the classes are very irregular. I observed also a considerable diversity of intellectual strength in the children.

A summary of the working of the institution from its foundation may be found in the following note, transcribed from the last published annual report :—

To 30th September last, there have been 131 children received—112 deaf and dumb and 19 blind ; 60 have been returned : 6 were found idiotic and beyond the influence of education—these were removed to asylums for the insane : 1 died ; 66 remained at date in the school. In 15 families, two or more were deaf mutes. 108 came from New South Wales, 17 from Queensland, 2 from New Zealand, 3 from Tasmania, and 1 from South Australia.

The balance-sheet for last year shows that the public subscribed a sum of £1428 18s. 9d., and that a further amount of £453 1s. 9d. was received for school fees and clothing. This is in most favourable contrast to the results shown by most of our other charitable institutions, where the difference between respective amounts of subscriptions and payments as compared with the Government subsidy is very discouraging.

COMPOSITION BY THE PUPILS.

The following specimens of composition, or essays are the work of some of the elder pupils, (the subjects are of their own choosing) and receive no correction except such as their respective writers can make on a careful review, when the prominent errors are pointed out by a Teacher. In judging them it is well to remember the ages of the writers, and the length of time at school. And that very few if any had acquired a knowledge of written or spoken language previously to their admission into the Institution.

By A. W.

THE WAR IN TURKEY.

There is now a dreadful war between Turkey and Russia. The Turks were very cruel to the poor christians some time ago and burnt their houses and killed the people. The Christians in Bulgaria and Servia suffered much. The former wicked Sultan killed himself. Mr. Gladstone was very angry with the Turks on account of their cruelty and he wrote a book about the persecution against the Christians. Many English people were very angry with Mr. Disraeli because he favoured the Turks as did Lord Derby. The religion of the Turks is Mahommedanism. The Turks will be defeated soon I think and I shall not be sorry for them. The Russians felt angry and began to fight against the Turks. We read in the newspaper that the Russians are very powerful under the General Gourdki. The Russians have large territory and population. The English people refused to go and fight against Russia to aid the Turks. It is very sinful to kill the Christians. All men are brothers and sisters on account of being descended from our first parents Adam and Eve. We hope that there will be no more war in the world soon, according to Isaiah's prophecy. Formerly king Edgar was called " The peaceable," because there was no war in his reign. There are between 12,000 and 15,000 Christian people in Turkey. We hope that the Russians and the Turks will become friends with each other. Richard I the great Crusader was obliged to make peace with Saladin because he did not want to fight more, so they made friends. Saladin was an enemy of the Christians, but he was kind to Richard I when he was sick, and sent him nice fruits.

By C. J.

ABOUT OUR TRIP TO GLADESVILLE.

We had holidays last July. We went by the bus to the Wharf at King street. Mr. Jeanneret kindly invited us to go there. We sat on his steamer going to Gladesville. We reached it at 11 o'clock. We walked on the road and through the bush. We played rounders and other games. We ate fruits and other nice things. We walked through the bush to the Lunatic

Asylum, and saw their large gardens. They have oranges and other fruits growing on the trees. It was nice to see all this. A man kindly gave us oranges. We felt much obliged to him for his kindness. We saw a large tortoise which was covered with its shell; also nice geese which came from Ceylon; also many birds in a large aviary. The poor lunatics have lost their reason. We pity them. We are thankful to God for our reason. But some people are apt to neglect to thank God for their reason. We entered the Asylum and saw their large dining rooms, kitchens, and other rooms. The keepers watch and teach the mad men as they dig up the garden. The Asylum is a nice building made of stone. Dr. Manning is over it. I did not see him because ho was away. I liked to see Gladesville. It is near Parramatta. There are many trees and other plants there. We returned here at 7 o'clock. We feel very thankful to Mr. Jeanneret for his great kindness also to other kind people.

By A. J.

AUTOUR L'EGLISE.

L'eglise est la maison de priere. Elle est une tres grande et belle place. Il y a plusieurs d'eglises a la campagne. Voila une eglise petite dans Watson's Bay. La Cathedrale est la plus grande de tous les eglises. La Cathedrale de St. Paul dans Londres est tres grande. C' etait batie a Monsieur Christopher Wren. Il etait un homme tres habile et bon. Il demeure dans le regne de Guillaume troisieme. Monsieur Hungerford est notre pasteur parceque Monsieur Taylor a alle a Londres. Les peuples allaient a l'eglise dernier Dimanche. Ils lissent le sainte Bible, Hymnes et prieres livres. Monsieur R. T. est alle a Anglais. Les peuples lui aiment tres beaucoup. Il venera a Sydney prochain annee. Il venera dans un grand Vaisseau. Jesus Christ est la tete de l'eglise qui est utile faite honneur de Notre Pere qui est dans le ceil. Voila sept eglises dans Asie a qui l'apostle Jean ecrivait. Leurs noms sont a Ephese, Smyrne, Pergame, Thyatire, Sardes, Philadelphie et Laedicee. Les peuples louent Dieu. L'eglise est faite des pierres et des bois. Quelque sont hauts et grands mais les autres sont petit et plaines. Dieu regle audessus les eglises et tous les hommes. Nous ne jouons pas ici sur le Dimanche. Les peuples ecoutent autour le sermon. Nous n' il ecoutons pas parceque nous sommes sourds muets. On n'allent pas a l'eglise parcequ 'ils sont malades et pauvres. L'eglise de St. Paul a Londres etait detrui a une grande feu. Elle a un tour et beaucoup d' ornements. Elle a fenetres beaux. J'ai besoin il voir, mais je ne peus pas y aller.

By H. C. S.

ABOUT TRICKETT AND RUSH.

E. Trickett the champion rower, was born at Greenwich near the Parramatta River. His height is 6 feet 3½ inches. His parents lived with him in a humble cottage when he was young. He was very fond of learning how to row. He continued to do so when he grew up to be a man. He often rowed well at the races because his muscles are very strong. Trickett was defeated some years ago by Rush and Conlan in a double scull match. He once won with his brother the double scull race for youths under twenty-one at the Anniversary regatta. E. Trickett had a match with E. McClees in light skiffs, and beat him nine years ago. He won other races. He went to England, and in June 1876 he pulled on the Thames against Sadler, then the champion rower and beat him easily. Trickett rowed against Rush on the

Parramatta River last June 1877 and got the medal &c. Rush was defeated. Trickett's friends wore blue ribbons. Rush's wore green ribbons. He lives at an hotel in Pitt-street in Sydney. He is 26 years of age. M. Rush was born at Tyrone in Ireland. His height is 6 feet and weight 15 stone. He is 33 years of age. He lives near the Clarence river. He once defeated Conlan. Another Clarence man with Rush rowed against the brothers Trickett in a double scull race for £50 and won, defeating the brothers easily. Rush lives at Grafton and keeps a store. Some of the Elder D and D went to see the races and we enjoyed it greatly. Many thousands of people went there. Mr. Kelly and the gentlemen of the rowing club kindly let us sit in their ground.

By D. J.

AUTOUR L'ECOLE.

L'ecole est tres utile et bonne. J'aime l'ecole parcqu'-elle est utile et belle. Les garcons et moi apprendons lo Sainte Bible et la Geographie, et l'historie de l'Anglais, grammaire, le troisieme livre et autres aussi. Deux garcons et moi aimons apprendre l'Francais livres, mais il est tres difficile. Nous avons toujours a lire les livres tous les nuits. Les livres sont dans notre librairie. Les docteurs nous instruissent les lecons utiles. Quatre garcons et moi sont desseinant sur la papier tous les Mardi et les Jeudi. Mademoiselle Sharp est notre maitresse de desscin. Nous sommes tres heureuse parceque le annual assemblage sera bientot. Les filles et les garcons ecrivent sur le planche noir. Les peuples aiment a voir ces pupitres. Je pense que notre goubern ator Monsieur H. R. sera le president. Il est un homme sage. Nous avons un vache et un chat, un chien et les poulets dans notre champs. Nous avions les lapins, mais nous n' en avons pas a present. Les garcous aiment jeur a travers le champs. Ils aiment jour a le ballon tous les jours. Nous remercons Dieu pour l'education. Je pense tous les garcons aiment etudier les lecons. Les committee des dames toujours venent ici tous les mois. Nous avons deux belle instruments de musique dans notre committee chambro. Les garcons aiment a lire la gazette tous les matins. Nous lissons toujours la siante Bible. Nous il aimons tres beaucoup. Docteur R. est un homme tres bon aussi Monsieur J. Nous sommes tres reconnaisant a ces hommes.

By H. B.

ABOUT THE BIBLE.

The Bible is the best book. It is the holy word of God. It is divided into two parts called the Old and New Testament. There are thirty-nine books in the Old Testament, and twenty-seven in the New Testament. There are sixty-six books in the whole Bible. Holy men inspired by God wrote it. The old testament books were collected and arranged by Ezra the priest. The Old Testament was written before the coming of Christ. The New Testament was written after Christ's death. It tells us about the birth, life, death, and ascension of Christ. There were twelve minor prophets, namely Jonah, Zephaniah, Hosea, Amos, Joel, Obadiah, Micah, Nahum, Habakkuk, Haggai, Zechariah, and Malachi. There were four great prophets, namely Isaiah, Jeremiah, Ezekiel, Daniel. There are five books in it called the Pentateuch which Moses wrote,—namely Genesis, Exodus, Leviticus, Numbers and Deuteronomy. There are four gospels namely Matthew, Mark, Luke and John. Athelstan, Wickliffe, Cranmer, and others translated the Bible. Forty-seven divines translated the Bible as we now have it A.D 1607 till 1610. The Bible is translated now into many different languages. The language of China is difficult, so are other foreign tongues. Timothy's mother taught him to read the Scriptures. The missionaries pity and teach the heathen about God and Christ. The missionaries translate the Bible for the heathen. The Bible says "the heaven and the Earth shall pass away but the word of God shall not pass away." It also tells us "there shall be a new heaven and a new earth where sin shall never enter." The Psalms are the sweet songs of the Bible. David and other good men wrote the Psalms. Many people love the Bible very much. Bad people do not want to read the Bible.

By M. J. G.

MARY AND HER LITTLE FRIEND.

Mary was a little orphan. She had a father and mother who loved her very dearly, but God took them away to a better world and she was lonely. She cried very sadly for having lost her parents. When she laid her head on the pillow at night she often sobbed herself to sleep. She was a little servant girl with her old mistress, who made her work very hard though she was only twelve years of ago. She was often unkind to Mary. She became acquainted with a little pet bird called robin and it made her happy. One day she found the robin on the ground, and it was nearly dead with cold. She put it in her bosom to try and warm its little heart. It was able to stand on the table on which Mary set it. Mary put it in the old cage instead of a goldfinch which had died. She was very kind to give it food and water always. She shut the door of the cage at first, but one day she left it open and the robin flew off. It was so tame that it stood on the table and picked the loaf. By and by it grew tamer, and then Mary left the door and window open. It stayed with her without fear. When the snow was gone away the robin flew off to the country. It often came to see her. In the summer the robin built its nest near the house. This teaches us to be kind to the lower animals, which were all made by God. If we are kind to them then God is pleased with us. God takes care of them and supports them. He loves us more than the lower animals because we have reason, and because we were made in his image at first. God will be angry at us if we are unkind to the lower animals. We ought to be thankful to God for His goodness. We should show our gratitude by loving and serving God and being kind always.

By A. McD.

ATOUR CASTLE HILL.

Mes grands parents demeurent dans Castle Hill. Ils sont tres bons. Ils ont beaucoup de fruits, moutons, chevaux, vaches, et chiens. J'aime Castle Hill. Castle Hill est autour sept milles de Paramatta. Paramatta est remarquable pour les bons oranges &c. Castle Hill est entre Paramatta et Dural. J'etais ne a Concord pres Paramatta riviere. Ma mere est morte. Mon pere et mon frere demeurent a Concord. Je les aime. Mon pere est appele Monsieur McDonald. Ils nous donnent beaucoup d'oranges souvent. Ils ont plusieurs d'amis. Il y a une eglise de Angleterre et une Wesleyan a Castle Hill. L'eglise de Angleterre est plus grand que l'eglise do Wesleyan. Il y a un Refuge a Paramatta pour les pauvres et pour les enfants et pour les lunatiques. Paramatta n'est pas grand, mais il est jolie. Il est quartorize milles do Syduoy. Ma tante demeure a Waterloo et elle est tres bonue. Le ville de Sydney est plus grand que Paramatta. Il y a dans Sydney un Halle, Cathedral, General Post Office, College, Universitie, Infirmary, Le College est pres notre Institution, aussi le Universite. Les etudiants apprendons dans la Universite. Ils aiment apprendre le livres. Le Universite est plus grand quo la College. Captain Cook trouve Botany Bay A.D. 1770. Il etait un hommes tres bon et bonte. Il etait ne a Yorkshire dans Angleterre. Il etait tue a uoirs hommes a Haivu iles. Ils etaient tres mauvaises et ignorants. Il etait compagne avec Monsieur Josephine Banks, qui etait un Botaniste. Il trouve les fleurs a Botany Bay. Monsieur Philip etait le premier gouverneur de N. S. Wales. Il etait un homme tres grand. Il demeurait dans Sydney. Il y a fleurs, oiseaux, animaux, &c., dans Botanic Gardens. Nous aimons voir les Jardins Botanics. Le population de Sydney est autour 160,000 que est plus grand que Brisbane, mais Melbourne est le plus grand.

By E. D. C.
ABOUT AFFLICTION.

Affliction is poverty, disease, the loss of friends, and other trials. God lays affliction on men. Why? For their good. Affliction came into the world when Adam and Eve had sinned. Sin causes trials and sufferings. All men suffer. Both good and bad must endure affliction. God afflicts the righteous to humble them before Himself, to try their faith, and to promote His own glory. God afflicts the wicked as a punishment for their sin, and to show His own justice. Job when tried said, " Naked came I out of my mother's womb and naked shall I return thither; the Lord gave and the Lord hath taken away; blessed be the name of the Lord." Eli when in anxiety said, " It is the Lord, let him do what seemeth Him good." We should learn to hate sin and to love holiness. We should call upon the Lord in our tribulation. David said, " Before I was afflicted I went astray, but now have I kept Thy word. It is good for me that I have been afflicted." Job says, " To him that is afflicted pity should be shewn from his friends." There shall be no sorrow or trials in heaven. Because there will be no sin in heaven.

SPEECHES AND PROCEEDINGS

AT THE

SIXTEENTH ANNUAL PUBLIC MEETING.

Extracted from the daily Press.

The Sixteenth annual meeting of the subscribers to the New South Wales Institution for the Deaf and Dumb and the Blind was held at the Asylum, Newtown Road, yesterday afternoon. The School Room had been newly coloured and had a bright and cheerful appearance, was hung round with drawings and fern pictures the work of the children. There was a very large attendance of ladies and gentlemen interested in the institution. His Excellency Sir Hercules Robinson presided. Among those present were Captain and Mrs. St. John, Revs. Dr. Lang, G. King, S. Wilkinson, H. Macredie, C. Olden, S. Hungerford, W. Scott, W. Bradley, Hon. A. Levy, M.L.C., Fiji ; Messrs. J. Henry, Hugh Robison, G. A. Lloyd, M.L.A., J. Mills, J. Paxton, J.P., Ellis Robinson, J. Haylock, E. Saber, M. Levy, Rev. W. Hough, and Mr. Thomas. Among the ladies present were Mrs. Goodlet, Mrs. Baillie, Mrs. Lang, Mrs. Levy, Mrs. King, Mrs. Love, Miss Mackie, Mrs. and Miss Holt, Mrs. Threlkeld, and Mrs. Macgregor.

His EXCELLENCY, in opening the proceedings, said : Ladies and Gentlemen,—It affords me much gratification to be present once more at the annual meeting of the New South Wales Institution for the Deaf and Dumb and the Blind. Five years have elapsed since I first presided here over a gathering similar to the present, and in the interval I have marked with much satisfaction the firm and increasing hold which this excellent institution has taken upon the sympathy and liberality of the public of New South Wales. The result has been that this institution has steadily advanced in efficiency, and has been enabled year by year to extend the sphere of its operations and of its usefulness. The annual report which is about to be laid before you shows that the transactions of the past year have been quite as favourable as those of any year that preceded it. The health of the pupils has been more than usually good. Their educational progress has been satisfactory. The number of the inmates has been maintained at 70—one in excess of the previous year—whilst the increases which have taken place both in subscriptions and the school fees has enabled the committee not only to meet the current expenditure, but also to carry out many very desirable improvements without incurring any considerable debt. These are results on which I may fairly congratulate all present. (Cheers.) And I think that they evince a careful solicitude and watchfulness of the interests of this institution on the part of all those engaged in its management, which entitles them to our warmest thanks. I will now call upon the hon. secretary to read the annual report. (Cheers.)

Mr. Ellis Robinson (hon. secretary) then read the Report, to be found on previous pages.

In the absence of the hon. Treasurer through illness, the hon. secretary read a balance-sheet, following items :—The subscriptions and donations from the public amounted to £728 18s.; amount received for school fees, £433 12s. 9d.; repayments by parents for clothing, £130 6s. 3d.; collected in New South Wales by Mr. Luff, £800 1s.; other collections, £42 19s. 6d.; legacy, late Charles Button, £50 ; grant from Government £450 ; W. B. Campbell's golden barrel, £100 10s. 11d. ; donation from employees Northern Railway, Queensland, £33 4s. ; and sundry other amounts to debit of income, making £2,862 11s. 4d. in all. On the side of expenditure, there is the sum of £750 17s. for salaries, &c. ; provisions, £549 13s. 6d. ; furniture, repairs, &c., £234 7s. 7d. ; clothing, &c., £211 7s. 11d. ; advertising and printing, £153 6s. 3d. ; commission, &c., £313 14s.; transferred to building fund, for wall, £300 ; and sundry amounts, leaving £130 14s. 5d. to credit in the bank. There is still, however, a liability to be met of about £247 10s. for erection of iron railing and gates, &c.

Rev. G. King moved the adoption of the report and balance-sheet. He remarked that they had often had occasion to congratulate the friends and supporters of this institution on the result of the year's work, which they came there periodically to review. He was happy to be able to state that the present was not an exception to the general rule. Eleven additional pupils had been received during the year, and twelve had left, having completed their education. It was to this latter class that they must look in forming an estimate of the success of that institution, and it was not merely the number that have been educated within those walls that constituted the criterion of their success—they must look also to the kind of education imparted, to the character and the discipline exercised over them, and the utility of the industrial habits which they have learned. They received pupils in all their native deficiency, both the blind and the deaf and dumb, their object being to raise up a structure of moral, intellectual, and industrial manhood. In each case new faculties have to be created, and when formed are to be educated and directed both for this world and that which is to come. In their review of this great work they had felt their own powerlessness, and they acknowledged that their sufficiency was altogether of God. With reference to the educational acquirements of the pupils those present would be able to form an estimate for themselves by the examination which was to be held in their presence, and they were at liberty to ask any questions they pleased on the various subjects set down in the programme. And with regard to the industrial habits of the children he would observe that the pupils, both male and female, were engaged during a portion of the day in industrial pursuits connected with the management of the household affairs there, and in the adjoining grounds, besides which the boys learn trades as far as practicable, and the girls learn dressmaking. Four pupils had thus been educated, and are now able to maintain themselves by the labour of their own hands. A fifth had recently been apprenticed to the trade of chair-caning, and having expressed a desire to learn basket-making also, that desire he was happy to say had been gratified by the kindness of a lady, who had contributed the required amount of fees. That was an example which he trusted would be followed by many. He regarded the acquisition of industrial habits, and the learning of trades there as a very important branch of the education of the children in that institution. (Hear, hear.) He hoped the time was not far distant when they would have an opportunity to devote more constant attention to industrial pursuits than they had been hitherto able to do. Many well-disposed persons when solicited for a contribution to such a charitable cause, excused themselves by saying "protect us from imposition and we will support you to the utmost of our power." To such persons he could confidently recommend that institution. There could be no imposition there. There, in every case, both of the blind and the deaf and dumb, they marked the hand of Divine Providence. Neither of those afflictions arose from any fault of the children themselves, or of their parents. Whatever the cause that one result they clearly perceived ; in it they beheld the hand of Divine Providence, taking each of those afflicted children and leading them to the door of that institution and commending them to the tender care of His more favoured children, and thus give them an opportunity of ministering to their wants by an appropriate education, and furnishing them with some equivalent for the loss of those senses which nature had so mysteriously denied to them and what higher privilege could be conferred on mortals here below than that of supplementing the deficiencies of nature by the education imparted here. They raised up those afflicted children from their native state of ignorance and helplessness to become intellectual and industrious ; to be able to maintain themselves by the labour of their own hands, and to attain the grand end of man's being, both as members of society here, and heirs of immortality hereafter. That was an object worthy of the highest beneficence. That was an institution to which every individual in the community might conscientiously contribute, for it was absolutely free from all sectarianism and in its nature and character purely charitable. He should not occupy their time any longer, but begged to move the adoption of the report. (Applause.)

Mr. M. LEVY, J.P., seconded the motion, and expressed his delight at seeing the meeting so numerously attended, especially by the ladies. He also had great pleasure at seeing the advancement made by the afflicted pupils.

The motion was carried unanimously.

Rev. Dr. LANG said having been identified with that institution from its origin he had witnessed its gradual advancement and its present condition with very great pleasure indeed. On one occasion when it was in a much earlier state of progress than it had now attained to, he was sent with others by the office-bearers to Sir Charles Cowper, who was then Premier, and who was well affected to the institution and to himself at the time, expecting that he would only succeed in getting 2½ acres of land, being one-half the extent there was then available in that locality. He found Sir Charles, however in a very good mood, and favourably disposed both to the institution and to himself, and by reasoning a little on the subject he got Sir Charles to give them the whole five acres which were now the property of the institution. He had had great pleasure in observing the gradual advancement of the institution to its present condition, and the great benefit it had conferred under its very worthy agent Mr. Watson, and the other officers. They, the Committee, had not only rendered great service to the afflicted of New South Wales, but they had also extended the assistance to the neighbouring colonies of Queensland, and New Zealand, and even Tasmania, and they had now a greater body of beneficiaries to present to the public as the result of the labours of that institution ; assisted as they had been by a generous public. The audience were aware that a large portion of the expenditure of the institution was provided from the contributions of the Government and Parliament of the colony. The annual donation from this source at present was £450, and the debt he had to discharge was to propose,—"That the thanks of this meeting are hereby given to the Government and Parliament for the annual donation of £450, in aid of the funds of the institution."

Rev. W. Scott seconded the resolution, which was carried unanimously.

Rev. S. Wilkinson moved,—"That the following gentlemen do constitute the committee for the ensuing year :—President, the Rev. George King, M.A. ; Vice-president, Rev. Dr. Lang ; Hon. Treasurer, Mr. Henry Phillips ; Hon. Secretary, Mr. Ellis Robinson ; Hon. Surgeon, Mr. Arthur Renwick, M.D. ; committee, Mr. E. T. Beilby, Mr. S. C. Brown, M.L.A., Hon John Frazer, M.L.C. Mr. J. R. Fairfax, Mr. Robert Hills, Mr. James Henry, Mr. J. R. Linsley, J.P., Rev. James Milne, M.A., Mr. F. R. Robinson, Mr. George F. Wise, Mr. J. R. Love, Mr. Joseph Paxton, Mr. E. Saber, Rev. W. Scott, Mr. John Mills."

Rev. H. Macreadie seconded the resolution, which was agreed to without dissent.

A vote of thanks to his Excellency for presiding was carried unanimously.

Several pieces of music were sung and performed on the piano and harmonium by the blind pupils, in a manner that evinced the great pains taken with them by their teacher Miss Sharpe. Children, both blind, and deaf and dumb, were then examined in several subjects of instruction by Mr. Watson, and their answers showed considerable proficiency and intelligence. All the children looked exceedingly clean, healthy, and happy, and their demeanour towards their teachers indicated love and gratitude ; they all appeared pleased at being the objects of so much attention, and this feeling was expressed by one of the mute girls in writing on the black-board in language well chosen and appropriate to the occasion.

The National Anthem was sung by the blind children, after which the meeting terminated.

Sydney, 30th September, 1877.

HENRY PHILLIPS, *Hon. Treasurer, in a/c with* N.S.W. INSTITUTION FOR THE DEAF & DUMB, & THE BLIND.

Dr. GENERAL FUND ACCOUNT. Cr.

INCOME.	£	s.	d.
To Balance at credit in Commercial Bank as per last year's account	9	18	8
,, Subscriptions and Donations (public)	728	18	0
,, Amount received for School Fees	433	12	9
,, Re-payments for Clothing by Parents	130	6	3
,, Amount of Collections in (N. S. W.) Country Districts by Mr. Luff, as per lists	800	1	0
,, Collected by the following:—			
W. G. O'Neil, Queanbeyan	26	4	0
Mr. Wilbow, Moonby	7	2	6
J. B. Wood, Grenfell	6	15	0
D. Capel, Piedmont	2	18	0
,, Received from Executors late Chas. Button, Legacy	50	0	0
,, Grant from N.S.W. Government for 1876	450	0	0
,, Interest received on investment J. W. Wood's Legacy	45	17	3
,, Amount Collected in Visitors Box at the Institution	3	2	6
,, 11th proportion of W. B. Campbell, proceeds "Golden Barrel"	100	10	11
,, Donation part proceeds, sale School of Arts property, Penrith	5	0	0
,, Donation from employees Northern Railway Queensland	33	4	0
,, Amount for sale of horse, saddle, and bridle	8	10	6
,, ,, ,, range	9	0	0
,, ,, ,, an organ	10	0	0
	£2,860	11	4
To Balance brought down being Amount at credit in Commercial Bank	130	14	5

EXPENDITURE.	£	s.	d.
By Salaries, labour, &c.	750	17	0
,, Provisions, Groceries, &c.	519	13	6
,, Furniture, additions, alterations, repairs	234	7	7
,, Drapery, Clothing, Boots, Bedding, &c.	211	7	11
,, Fuel, lighting, and medicine	68	16	0
,, Advertising, printing, stationery, and printing annual report	153	6	3
,, Sundries, petty house expenses, &c.	25	11	6
,, Wire fencing, &c.	17	15	8
,, Commission, collecting expenses, stamps, &c.	343	14	0
,, Books, Desks, and School requisites, &c.	64	12	6
,, Insurance on Buildings and Furniture	4	15	0
,, Transfer to Building Fund for wall, &c.	300	0	0
,, Half premium paid for Apprenticeship Fee	5	0	0
,, Balance, being amount at credit in Commercial Bank	130	14	5
	£2,860	11	4

NOTE.—Liabilities—Erection of Iron Railing and Gates, Architects Commission ... £247 10 0

E. & O. E, Sydney, 29th September, 1877.

HENRY PHILLIPS, *Hon. Treasurer.*

Audited and found correct,

JOHN F. PAIGE,
W. H. MACKENZIE, SEN. } *Auditors.*

October 4th, 1877.

Sydney, 30th September, 1877.

HENRY PHILLIPS, *Hon. Treasurer in a/c with* N.S.W. INSTITUTION FOR THE DEAF & DUMB, & THE BLIND.

Dr.   BUILDING FUND ACCOUNT.   **Cr.**

INCOME.	£	s.	d.	EXPENDITURE.	£	s.	d.
To Balance of last year's account in Commercial Bank	419	18	5	By Payments to Contractor for erection of stone wall and gate piers, &c.	750	0	0
" Bequest of the late Mrs. Sarah White	50	0	0	" Balance in Commercial Bank to credit	19	18	5
" Transfer from General Fund a/c	300	0	0				
	£769	18	5		£769	18	5
To Balance brought down being amount at credit in Commercial Bank	19	18	5				

Audited and found correct,
JOHN F. PAIGE,
W. H. MACKENZIE, SEN. } *Auditors.*
4th October, 1877.

E. & O. E.
Sydney, 29th September, 1877.
HENRY PHILLIPS, *Hon. Treasurer.*

PERPETUAL SUBSCRIBERS' FUND ACCOUNT.

TRUSTEES—REV. G. KING, *President;* HENRY PHILLIPS, *Hon. Treasurer;* ELLIS ROBINSON, *Hon. Secretary.*

	£	s.	d.		£	s.	d.
To amount Legacy received from the late John W. Wood, of Glebe Point	1000	0	0	By Purchase of N. S. Wales 5 per cent. Debentures, one of......£500 0 0 Four, each £100.... 400 0 0	900	0	0
				" Premium paid on same 6¼ per cent.	58	10	0
				" Balance deposited in Savings Bank to credit of the Institution, as per Pass Book	41	10	0
	£1,000	0	0		£1,000	0	0

E. & O. E.
Sydney, 29th September, 1877.
HENRY PHILLIPS, *Hon. Treasurer.*

Audited and found correct,
JOHN F. PAIGE,
W. H. MACKENZIE, SEN. } *Auditors.*
4th October, 1877.

Annual Subscriptions, Donations, &c.

Received for the year ending 30th September, 1877.

——————:o:——————

☞ N.B.—It is particularly requested that should any omission or inaccuracy appear in this list it be notified to the Secretary for correction.

	£	s.	d.		£	s.	d.
				Baird, Thomas, Dubbo ...	£1	0	0
Ashcroft, James, Cannonbar	1	0	0	Boucher, J.. Cooma ...	1	1	0
Anonymous	0	2	6	Bonynge, T., Wagga Wagga	1	0	0
Alexander, Mrs. M.... ...	1	1	0	Barnes, J. and E. " Coota-			
Allan, H. E. A.	1	0	0	mundra," 1876	1	0	0
Anderson, D.	0	10	0	Baines, H., Casino	1	0	0
Anderson, James	0	10	0	Brown, Mrs. J. H.	1	1	0
Alderson and Sons	1	1	0	Ball, John, " Minchec,"			
Allt and Co.	1	1	0	Gundagai	0	10	0
Abigail, F.	0	10	0	Baillie, Mrs. J. H.	2	2	0
Allwood, Rev. Canon ...	1	1	0	Bown, Charles	1	1	0
Atherden, George	2	2	0	Brown, S. C., M.P.	2	2	0
Aitken, T....	1	1	0	Beilby, E. T.	2	2	0
Abronson, H., Cundletown	1	1	0	Brown, Andrew, J.P.			
Allan, J. T., Goulburn ...	1	0	0	Lithgow	2	0	0
Anderson and Co., Pitt-				Baylis, E....	0	10	0
street	1	1	0	Brereton, Dr. Le Gay ...	2	2	0
Aarons, J. J. P., "Nanima"				Berry, D. " Coolangatta,"			
Wellington	1	1	0	Shoalhaven, 1876-7 ...	2	2	0
Albery, Mark	1	1	0	Burton, J....	0	10	6
Allerding, F. and Son ...	1	1	0	Bull, W., J.P.	1	1	0
Allen, Sir George Wigram	2	2	0	Butler, E., Q.C. M.P. ...	1	1	0
Alcock, Mrs., per Mrs.				Baker, Thomas	1	1	0
Hellier	1	1	0	Bennett, S.	1	1	0
Abbey, W.	1	0	0	Buchanan, W. F.	1	1	0
Alger, J.	1	1	0	Broadhurst, Mrs.	1	1	0
				Bauss, C. J. H.	1	1	0
Button, Charles (Legacy)	50	0	0	Blomfield, R. H., Mac-			
Breillat, Mrs., Annandale,				quarie Fields	1	1	0
1876	1	1	0	Buchanan, B. (Mort & Co.)	2	2	0
Brocklehurst, W. W., Lon-				Barton, Mrs. Edward, Wal-			
don, per Wolfen and Co.	5	0	0	lerawang	2	0	0
Biss, Mrs. (Quarterly) ...	1	0	0	Bird, H. S.	1	1	0
Broughton, Robert, don-				Butler, W., Kilcoy, Bris-			
ation	5	0	0	bane	2	2	0

Name	£	s	d
Bradley, Newton, and Lamb	£1	1	0
Binney, R.	2	2	0
Barker, Right Rev. Dr., Bishop of Sydney	2	2	0
Breillat, Mrs., Annandale	1	0	0
Brown and Co.	1	1	0
Butterworth, Henry, Bathurst	1	1	0
Bowman, Mrs. W., Windsor	2	0	0
Bowman, Miss, ditto	1	0	0
Bowman, G. J.P., ditto	5	5	0
Bransby, C. S., Moss Vale	1	1	0
Badgery, Henry, J.P., Vine Lodge, Sutton Forest	1	1	0
Bates, Miss Emma	2	0	0
Barnos, J. and E., Cootamundra	1	0	0
Boles, W.	1	1	0
Bootes, W., Gundagai	1	0	0
Barker, Rev. H., Sutton Forest	1	0	0
Begg, John E.	1	1	0
Barnard and Hinton	1	1	0
Betts, Miss, Glebe Point Road	2	2	0
Bell, Henry	1	1	0
Bayly, N. P., "Havelah" Mudgee	5	0	0
Buzacott and Armstrong	1	1	0
Biddell Bros.	0	10	6
Brush, John	1	1	0
Bright Bros. and Co	2	2	0
Bond, C. B.	1	1	0
Blackburn and Co.	1	1	0
Bryen, S. J.	1	1	0
Campbell, W. B., (Golden Barrel)	100	10	11
Campbell, Archibald, Lorn Bank, Macquarie Plains	1	1	0
Cox, Hon. G. H., M.L.C., "Burrandulla," Mudgee	2	2	0
Cameron, Mrs. E. W. "Ewenton," Balmain	2	2	0
Crane, G. E.	1	1	0
Cowper, Very Rev. Dean	1	0	0
Crane, W., J.P.	1	1	0
Callaghan and Son	1	1	0
Chapman, J. T.	1	1	0
Carss, W., Kogerah	1	0	0
Clarke, J.	0	5	0
Coghill, Mrs., per Robert Maddrell, Esq., "Bedervale," Braidwood	1	0	0
Carmichael, J.	£5	0	0
Cadell, Mrs., "Mullamuddy," Dubbo	1	0	0
Cox, A. H., J.P., "Wallingee," Mudgee	2	0	0
Camper, J. W.	0	5	0
Comrie, J., J.P., Kurragong	1	1	0
Campbell, Hon. Alexander, M.L.C., "Rosemount," Woollahra	2	2	0
Cohen Bros. and Co.	1	1	0
Clark, John, Market Wharf	1	1	0
Collins, E. E.	0	10	0
Critchley, Mrs. M. A., Darling Point	5	5	0
Chauvel, Mrs.	1	1	0
Chisholm, Mrs.	5	5	0
Codrington, J. F., Orange	1	1	0
Cameron, Alex., J.P., Rocky Mouth	1	0	0
Capel, D., J.P., "Piedmont," Barraba, Collected by—	2	8	0
Chisholm, John W., J.P., "Bredalbane," Goulburn	1	1	0
Campbell, John	0	10	0
Cooper, Nathan and Co.	1	1	0
Cook, Joseph	1	0	0
Clapham, R. W., Braidwood	1	1	0
Cram, P., Young	1	1	0
Clements, John and B. "Woolbrook" Bigga, Collected by—			
Clements, John	1	0	0
Clements, B.	1	0	0
Riddley, C.	1	0	0
Howard, John, Gum Flat	1	0	0
Howard, D. "	1	0	0
Five subscriptions 5s.	1	5	0
Four " 2s. 6d.	0	10	0
Day, Mrs., Senior, 1876-77	2	0	0
Donald, Rev. W. S., Clarence Town	1	1	0
Doran, Miss, 1876	1	1	0
Dearin, T. B.	3	0	0
Durham, Mrs.	1	1	0
Dight, Mrs. Arthur	1	0	0
Davidson, Murray, Cullen Bullen	1	0	0
Dixson and Sons	1	1	0
Durham, C.	2	2	0
Donnithorne, Miss, Newtown	1	1	0

	£	s	d
Daintrey, E.	£1	1	0
Darley, Hon. F. M.L.C.	1	1	0
Docker, A. R.	1	0	0
Day, William, J.P., "Western Lea," Pyrmont	1	0	0
Drummond, J. M., " Bookham," Yass	1	0	0
Doran, Miss	1	1	0
Dangar, H. C., M.P.	3	3	0
Dangar, Mrs. H. C.	1	1	0
Durham, J., Singleton	1	1	0
Davies, William, Goulburn	1	1	0
Docker, Hon. Joseph, M.L.C.	1	1	0
Donnelly, J. "Berambula," Wagga Wagga	1	0	0
Dickson, Mrs., Senior, Mudgee	1	1	0
Davis, R., Brisbane Water	1	1	0
Dudley, F. H. "Pegus," Goulburn	1	1	0
Dun, "Spiro," Spero	0	5	0
Dicker, Rev. Henry, " Coonabarabran "	1	1	0
Employees of Southern and Western Railway, Queensland, per Alfred Thomas, Esq.	33	4	0
Elouis, C.	2	2	0
Evans, Captain, Newtown (1876)	1	1	0
Ecclesiastes XI, 1 v.	0	5	0
Elliott Brothers	1	1	0
Evans, Captain, Newtown	1	1	0
Elliott, P. J. and Co.	1	1	0
Forsyth, George, J.P., Yarrangobilly, Tumut	1	1	0
Flower, Miss	1	1	0
Forsyth, A. and Co.	3	3	0
Friend, per Edward Knox, Esq.	0	5	0
Frazer, Mrs. Simon	0	10	0
Friend, per James Henry, Esq.	0	5	0
Fenwick, C. D.	1	1	0
Frazer, Mrs. Andrew	0	10	0
Fort street school pupils, per Mrs. Allingham, for books	5	5	0
Fairclough, Capt. Parramatta	1	1	0
Fache, C. J.	2	2	0
Fletcher, J., J.P., Walcha	2	2	0
Faucett, His Honor Judge	£1	1	0
Friend, W. S.	2	2	0
Farmer, and Company	1	1	0
Fairfax, James R.	1	1	0
Fairfax, Edward R.	1	1	0
Fairfax, Mrs. C.	2	0	0
Fairfax, John	0	10	0
Faithfull, W. P., J.P., " Springfield" Goulburn	2	2	0
Flavelle, Bros. and Roberts	1	1	0
Frost, Richard, Orange	1	0	0
Friedman, A.	1	1	0
Forsythe, J.	1	0	0
Ferguson, G.	1	1	0
Frazer, Hon. John, M.L.C.	5	5	0
Freemasons Lodge Woolloomooloo, No. 386 S.C. per R. Watson	2	2	0
Fitzpatrick, M., M.P.	1	0	0
Frazer, John and Company	3	3	0
Gay, E., Tamworth	0	10	0
Gill, John, J.P., Moonby	1	0	0
Garnsey, Rev. C. F.	1	1	0
Gill, G. R., J.P., Moonby	1	1	0
Gray, Son and Co.	1	1	0
Gamble, G.	1	0	0
Greenhill, S.	2	2	0
Gross, J. C. "Strathbogie," Vegetable Creek	1	1	0
Gibson, Frederick F. " Caragabell," Grenfell	1	1	0
Gennys, Mrs., Carcoar	1	0	0
Goodlet and Smith	2	2	0
Galloway, J., Parramatta	1	0	0
Geekie, Rev. Dr., Bathurst	1	0	0
Gardiner, John A., " Gabalion," Wellington	1	1	0
Griffiths and Co.	2	0	0
Giblin, V. W.	2	2	0
Gilchrist, Watt and Co.	1	1	0
Gibson, Andrew, J.P., " Tirama," Goulburn	1	1	0
Gordon, Hon. S. D., M.L.C.	1	0	0
Garavel, Rev. J. M.	1	1	0
Gorman, Henry	1	1	0
Gibson, L. L. " Longford," Bendemere	1	0	0
Gardiner, W. and Co.	2	2	0
Garrick and Co.	1	1	0
Graham, J., J.P.	1	1	0
Hay, Hon. John, M.L.C.	5	0	0
Haines, F. E., Castlestead Burrowa	1	0	0

Hammond, H. W.	£2	0	0
His Worship the Mayor of Sydney	2	2	0
Huxley, Mrs., Jerry's Plains	0	5	0
Hordern, L.	5	0	0
Hayley, E. W. S.	0	10	0
Hassall, Miss	1	0	0
Haylock, Dr., Enfield ...	1	1	0
Hoffnung, S. and Co. ...	1	1	0
Holle, J. F.	1	1	0
Holt, Hon. Thomas, M.L.C.	5	0	0
Hyam, M., J.P., Nowra ...	1	1	0
Hall, F., "Springfield," Waverley	1	1	0
Hobson, Mrs.	1	0	0
Hardy, Bros., Hunter st.	1	1	0
Hand, F., Bega	1	0	0
Hurley, John, Glebe ...	1	1	0
Hamburger, Bros. and Co.	2	2	0
Hamburger, M., donation	2	2	0
Hordern, E.	1	1	0
Holdsworth, J. B.	2	2	0
Humphery, Mrs. F. T., Double Bay, per Rev. G. King, towards apprenticeing a blind boy to a trade	5	0	0
Harris, William, Haymarket	1	1	0
Hezlet, W. J., J.P.... ...	0	10	6
Hezlet, Mrs.	0	10	6
Houison, Mrs., Parramatta	1	0	0
Holt, F. S. E.	1	1	0
Hills, Robert	1	1	0
Hume, A. Hamilton, J.P. "Everton" Rye Park, Donation	1	0	0
Howell, Mrs. P.	1	1	0
Henry, James, 754 George street	2	2	0
Hume, Mrs. Hamilton, Clifton Wood, Yass ..	1	0	0
Humphrey, F. T.	1	1	0
Harrison, Jones & Devlin	3	3	0
Hardy Bros., Oxford street	1	1	0
Hillier, Mrs.	1	1	0
Hardie, John	1	1	0
Humphery, C. H., Burwood	2	2	0
Harrison and Attwood ...	1	1	0
Hoskisson, Mrs. J., Windsor	1	0	0
Hawke, G., J.P., Byng ...	1	1	0
Hall, W. S., J.P., "Lilburn Hall" Windsor	1	0	0

Harriss, John, Thomasstreet, Ultimo	£2	2	0
Harriss, Miss M., Ultimo House, Ultimo	1	1	0
Harnett, Mrs. Mary, "Eucumbeno" Adaminaby...	1	0	0
Hindson, Lawrence	1	1	0
Harrison, J. S.	1	1	0
Iredale, L. F.	4	4	0
Jaye, James, Balmain ...	1	0	0
Josephson, J. F.	2	2	0
Josephson, His Honor Judge	2	2	0
Johnson, Rev. Thomas ...	1	0	0
Jenkins, Dr., J.P., Nepean Towers	5	0	0
Jones, Dr. P., Sydney ...	1	1	0
Jeffers, Miss	0	10	6
Jones, David and Co. ...	2	2	0
Jolly, W., J.P....	1	1	0
Kent, Mrs., "Elyston" Woollahra	10	10	0
Kenrick, A., Penrith ...	2	2	0
Keppie, W., Patterson ...	0	5	0
K. B. per G. King, Esq....	1	0	0
Knox, Edward	5	5	0
Keep, John and Co.... ...	1	1	0
Kemp, W. E.	2	0	0
Keep and Parsons	1	1	0
King, Rev. George, M.A., Burwood	1	0	0
Kinross, Rev., Principal, St. Andrew's College ...	1	1	0
Lambert, S., Tamworth ...	1	1	0
Liversedge, Professor, per Hon. Mrs. Hay	2	2	0
Leathes, A. Stanger... ...	2	2	0
Learmonth, Dickinson and Co., per G. F. Wise ...	1	1	0
Lester, Miss, Burwood ...	3	3	0
Leibius, Dr.	1	1	0
Laidley, W. and Co. ...	2	2	0
Lassetter, F. and Co. ...	1	1	0
Lord, E., City Treasurer	1	0	0
Looke, W., Balmain ...	1	0	0
Lamb, Mrs.	1	1	0
Linsley, J. R., J.P.	1	1	0
Levey, Montague, J.P. ...	1	1	0
Lester, W. R., Mudgee ...	1	0	0
Lorimer, Rome, and Co ...	1	1	0

	£	s.	d.
Lang, Rev. Dr.	1	1	0
Lowe, William H., "Eurundera," Mudgee	1	0	0
Lamb, Walter, J.P., "Quirang," Edgecliffe Road...	2	2	0
Love, J. R.	1	1	0
Lawson, G., Yass	1	0	0
Lovick, James and Co. ...	1	1	0
Milson, J., Jun., J.P. ...	3	3	0
May, Rev. W. North Goulburn, 1876	0	10	0
Millard, Rev. H. S., M.A., Newcastle	2	0	0
M. M. per S. Watson ...	1	0	0
Moffatt, S., Cumkillenbar	1	1	0
Marsh, Mrs., "Salisbury Court"	1	1	0
Manning, C. J....	2	2	0
Mansfield, G. Allen	1	1	0
Mitchell and Co.	1	1	0
"Missionary Glebe" per G. F. Wise...	1	0	0
Mills, John	1	1	0
Marks, John, J.P.	5	0	0
Milne, Rev. James, M.A...	1	0	0
Moore, E. L., Narellan ...	1	0	0
Montefiore, Joseph and Co.	1	1	0
Maxwell, E. C., "Southgate Mills," Clarence River	1	1	0
Merewether, Mrs., "The Ridge," Newcastle ...	3	3	0
Moore, C., J.P...	2	2	0
Macgregor, J.	1	1	0
Mackenzie, J. P.	1	0	0
Mort, Henry	2	2	0
Moses, Henry, M.P., Ashfield	1	0	0
Maddrell, Robert, J.P., "Bedervale," Braidwood	1	0	0
Mackellar, Dr....	1	0	0
Maxwell, A. H...	1	1	0
Miller, R.	0	10	6
Morehead, R. A. A.... ...	2	2	0
Moore, Thomas, Oxfordstreet	1	1	0
Myers and Solomon... ...	2	2	0
Maxwell, A. C....	1	1	0
Moore, W., 241, Elizabethstreet	1	0	0
Marina, Carlo, "Moppity," Young	1	0	0

	£	s.	d.
Mayor and Aldermen of the Municipal Council of Darlington, Annual Subscription	2	2	0
Manning, His Hon. Sir William...	1	1	0
Mason, Brothers	1	1	0
Mitchell, D. S., Darlinghurst road	2	0	0
Marsh, F., J.P., C.P.S., Wellington	0	10	0
Myers, J. H.	0	10	0
May, Rev. W., North Goulburn	0	10	0
Millett, E...	1	1	0
Metcalfe, Mrs....	1	1	0
Milson, J., 2nd subscription	3	3	0
McIntyre, Rev. D., "Tinonee" Manning river...	1	0	0
McIntosh, Alexander ...	1	1	0
MacPherson, Rev. P., East Maitland	1	1	0
McIntyre, D., "Kayuga"	1	0	0
McKay, D. F., Singleton...	1	0	0
McLean, John	0	10	0
McArthur and Co.	2	2	0
McDonald, Smith and Co.	1	0	0
MacDonnell, W.	0	10	6
McIntosh, J. N., Bathurst	1	0	0
McKillop, Duncan, "Terrabella" Dubbo	1	0	0
Neale, J. H., J.P.	1	1	0
N. P. C., Box, Post Office, Donation 1876	5	0	0
Nevison, A., J.P. Ohio ...	2	0	0
Nevison, J. A., Ohio ...	1	0	0
Nixon, W....	1	1	0
Nichol, D....	1	0	0
Nicholson, J., Bombala ...	1	0	0
Newman, J. Hubert ...	1	1	0
Newton, C, Bros. and Co.	2	2	0
Noake, J.	0	10	0
Norton, James	1	1	0
N. P. C.	5	0	0
O'Neill, W. G., Queanbeyan, Collected by—	26	4	0
Osborne, Miss, per F. P. McCabe, Esq., J.P. Wollongong	5	0	0
O'Reilly, Rev. Canon ...	1	0	0
Oriental Banking Co. ...	5	5	0

	£	s.	d.		£	s.	d.
Old, Richard, North Shore	2	0	0	Ralston, A. J.	1	1	0
O'Donnell, D. M. Vegetable				Ross, Mrs., Goulburn ...	1	0	0
Creek	1	0	0	Ryrie, S., "Cavan" Yass	1	0	0
				Rotton, H., J.P., "Black-			
Perry, John S.	10	0	0	down" Bathurst	1	1	0
Peate and Harcourt... ...	2	2	0	Roberts, W., Penrith ...	1	1	0
Potts, Mrs. J. H.	3	0	0	Richards, B., Windsor ...	1	1	0
Palser, H. P., J.P.	0	10	0	Robertson, T., Woollahra	1	1	0
Prince, Ogg and Co... ...	2	2	0	Robinson, F. R.	1	1	0
Perdriau, H., J.P.	1	1	0	Ritchie, W., Adelong ...	1	0	0
Plummer, James	1	1	0	Richardson and Wrench	2	2	0
Perry, W. and Co.	1	1	0	Roberts, Mrs. Mary	7	7	0
Perkins, Mrs. Thomas, Bal-				Rabone, Feez and Co. ...	1	1	0
main	1	1	0	Renwick, W. C.	2	2	0
Poolman, S.	1	1	0	Rankin, A. H., J.P., "Lock-			
Parbury and Lamb	1	1	0	yersleigh" Goulburn ...	1	1	0
Payne and Sanford, Braid-				Ross, J. Grafton	1	1	0
wood	1	1	0	Reading, Mrs. E.	1	1	0
Phillips, F...	1	1	0	Robinson, His Excellency			
Perks, F.	1	1	0	Sir Hercules, K.C.B., &c.	3	0	0
Pearson, S. J., Parramatta	2	2	0	Roberts, Mrs., "Harden			
Paige, J. F...	1	1	0	Villa" Young	2	2	0
Puddicombe, Very Rev.				Roseby, J....	0	10	0
Archdeacon, Goulburn	1	1	0				
Peck, Isaac	2	2	0	St. Stephen's Presbyterian			
Palmer, E. G. W.	0	10	0	Church, per A Dean ...	2	0	0
Peapes and Shaw	1	1	0	Stenkford, Mrs., St. Peter's,			
Phillips, Henry	1	1	0	Cook's River Road ...	1	0	0
Perrett, J., Tyringham ...	1	0	0	St. John's Lodge., I. O. O.			
				F. M. U., Donation per			
Quodling, Henry	2	2	0	Bro. Howe	5	0	0
				Sinclair, W., Wagga Wagga	2	2	0
Robinson, Mrs. G. L.				Smith, Ernest O.	1	1	0
Windsor, 1876	1	0	0	School Fines, Pyrmont ...	1	4	6
Raphael, J. G....	1	1	0	Smith, Thomas Hawkins,			
Ridge, M., Royal Circus,				Gordon Brook	1	1	0
Donation	2	0	0	Scott, Mrs. W., St. Paul's			
Renwick, Dr.	2	2	0	College	1	0	0
Roach, W. R.	1	1	0	Staff, Mrs. J. F.	1	0	0
Russell, H. C., B.A... ...	1	1	0	Savings	3	0	0
Robinson, Mrs. G. L.,				Salmon, J. G. "Bogandiua,"			
Windsor	1	0	0	Culgoa River, Collected			
Rush, Waltham	2	2	0	by—	7	13	6
Roberts, C. J.	0	10	0	Sly, J.	1	1	0
Ratnell, W., per M. Hyam,				Slade, G. P.	1	1	0
J.P., Nowra	1	1	0	Smith, R., (Slade & Smith)	2	2	0
Reeve, T. P.	1	0	0	Smith, Rev. Pierce Galliard,			
Rush, James, Sub-inspector	1	1	0	Canberra	1	1	0
Ryrie, David, J.P., "Cool-				Smart, Hon. T. W.,			
ringdon" Cooma... ...	2	2	0	M.L.C., "Mona" ...	2	2	0
Ross, Morgan and Co. ...	1	1	0	Sun Kum On	0	10	0
Roberts, T. J., "Exeter				Stephen, Sir Alfred, K.C.B.	1	0	0
Farm" Braidwood ...	1	0	0	Sands, John	1	1	0

Name	£	s	d
Stephen, M. H...	£3	0	0
Schultz, John, Eden ...	1	0	0
Skarratt, C. C....	1	1	0
Sloper, F. E.	1	1	0
Schuette, Dr. K.	1	1	0
Smyth and Wells	0	10	0
Smith, Hon. Dr., M.L.C.	1	1	0
Smith and Mannell... ...	1	1	0
Saber, W. and Sons ...	2	2	0
Stewart, Rev. Colin	1	0	0
Sharp, J. B., J.P. "Clifton Wood," Yass	1	1	0
Suttor, G. T. Baulkham Hills	1	0	0
Schlachter, F., Mudgee ...	1	0	0
Sheahan, J. R., Jugiong...	1	1	0
Smith, John, J.P. "Gamboola," Molong	1	1	0
Sigmont, F. M.	1	1	0
Scott, D.	1	1	0
Sparke, W. E....	1	1	0
Smyth, S. H.	2	2	0
Spring, James	1	1	0
Soul, Washington H. ...	1	1	0
Strickland, Josiah, "Bunderburra," Forbes ...	1	1	0
Street and Norton	1	1	0
Smith, Shepherd, N. S. W. Bank	10	0	0
Smith, Shepherd	2	2	0
Starkey, J....	1	1	0
Shadler, A...	1	1	0
Terry, R. R., Ryde	1	1	0
Threlkeld, Mrs., 1876 ...	1	1	0
Taylor, Henry J.	2	0	0
Tipping, John, donation, part proceeds sale of property, Penrith ...	5	0	0
Taylor, Mrs., "Terrible Vale"	1	1	0
Thomas, H. A., "Wivenhoe," Narellan	2	2	0
Thompson, R.	0	10	6
Trebeck, Mr. and Mrs. ...	1	1	0
Tucker and Co....	1	1	0
Thomas, T., Marrickville...	2	2	0
Trickett, W. J....	1	1	0
Tooth and Co.	2	2	0
Thorne, Mrs., "Prestonville"	2	2	0
Thurlow, C. A....	1	1	0
Thomson, Sir E. Deas, C.B., K.C.M.G.	1	1	0
Throsby, P. H., Moss Vale	£1	1	0
Thompson, E. H., C.P.S., Wagga Wagga	1	1	0
Thompson and Giles ...	2	2	0
Thompson, A., J.P.... ...	1	1	0
Tucker, W., J.P.	1	1	0
Thornton, George, J.P. ...	1	1	0
Teakle, C.	1	1	0
Tebbot and Co...	2	2	0
Tickle, J. B.	1	1	0
Threlkeld, Mrs...	1	1	0
Thomas, W., per E. Jeuner, Bookookarrara	0	10	0
Vickery, E.	2	0	0
Vallach, Mrs. W.	0	10	0
Verey, S. H. and G., Balmain	1	1	0
Voss, Houlton H., J.P., Union Club	2	2	0
Vaughen, Mrs. C. N. ...	0	10	0
Visitors Box	3	2	6
Walker, Thomas, Yarralla	10	0	0
Walker, Miss, ditto... ..	5	0	0
Warby, J....	0	5	0
Watson, Richard A.... ...	0	10	6
Warden, David, J.P., "Airlie House," Milton ...	1	1	0
Wilson, Rev. T., Randwick	1	1	0
Wilkinson, His Honor Judge	2	0	0
Wingate, Mrs.	1	1	0
Way, E.	1	1	0
Wilshire, F. R., P.M., Berrima...	1	0	0
Wren, Dr., Wagga Wagga	1	1	0
Wilkinson, W. T., Yass ...	1	1	0
White, Hon. James, M.L.C., "Cranbrook," Rose Bay	2	0	0
Wilson, S., Junee	1	0	0
Wearing, B. C...	1	1	0
Watson, John	1	1	0
Woolcott, W. P.	1	1	0
Woodward, F., Wollongong	1	1	0
Wise, George F.	1	1	0
Wilbow, George, Moonby, Collected by—			
Wilbow, G.	1	1	0
Wilbow, Mrs.	0	10	6
Kiss, G....	0	5	0
Giruey, C.	0	10	6
Buss, T....	0	2	6
Laidlow, Mrs.	0	5	0

	£	s.	d.
Dwyer, J.	0	2	6
Grant, A.	0	2	6
Spain, M.	0	2	6
McIlven, S.	0	2	6
Morrison, A....	0	5	0
Clark, J.	0	2	6
Jacob, J.	0	2	6
Orman, G.	0	2	6
Weaver, D.	0	5	0
Weaver, C.	0	2	6
Stuce, E.	0	2	6
Robson, J.	0	2	6
Miller, A.	0	4	0
Sage, Mrs.	0	3	0
Pulman, G.	0	10	6
Wilbow, J.	0	5	0
Barnes, K.	0	10	0
Barnes, W.	0	5	0
Matthews, W.	0	5	0
Chaffery, W....	0	5	0
Read, J....	0	3	0
McKennar, L.	0	2	6
	£7	2	6

Wood, J. B., Grenfell, Collected by—

	£	s.	d.
Wood, J. B....	1	1	0
Wilson, Rev. S.	1	1	0
Mitten, G., 1875	1	0	0
Mitten, G., 1876	1	0	0
Ryne, Mrs. D.	0	10	6
Gravenmaker, Mrs. ...	0	10	0
Buckman, J....	0	5	0
O'Connor, A. B.	0	5	0
Norris, J. W.	0	5	0
Burrell, H.	0	5	0
Johnstone, R.	0	5	0
McGrath, J. M.	0	5	0
Flecher, E.	0	2	6
	£6	15	0

	£	s.	d.
Young, James, South Creek	2	10	0
Young and Lark	1	1	0
Yates, L., J.P., C.P.S., Yass	1	1	0
Zollner, S....	0	10	6

☞ To Subscribers or Friends in the country districts who desire to help the Institution by collecting on behalf of the Funds, Subscription Lists or Cards will be forwarded on application to the Hon. Treasurer or Hon. Secretary—and the amounts received thankfully acknowledged.

Country Collections.

Per Mr. GEORGE LUFF.

NEW SOUTH WALES.

Various Towns are placed in alphabetical order.

Donations under 5s. are placed in Lump Sums.

ABERDEEN.

	£	s.	d.
Hall, G. P. " Blairmore "	1	0	0
Cundy, Mrs. G.	0	10	6
Hall, Mrs. G. P. " Blairmore "	0	10	0
Mackenzie, M. C.	0	10	0
McLean, J.	0	5	0

ARMIDALE.

	£	s.	d.
Lord Bishop of Grafton and Armidale Donation	2	2	0
Hargrave, Richard, J.P., Hill Grove	2	0	0
Proctor, W. C., Mayor	1	1	0
McDonald, R.	1	1	0
Thompson, J.	1	1	0
Moore, J., J.P.	1	1	0
Moore, Mrs. J.	1	1	0
Seabrook and Brown	1	1	0
White, Mrs.F.,"Saumarez"	1	0	0
Richardson, J. and Co.	1	0	0
Mallam, G. H., 1876-77	1	0	0
Blythe, Sydney, J.P.	1	0	0
Mutlow, W. H., 1876-77	1	0	0
Greaves, W. A. B.	1	0	0
Kendall, B.	1	0	0
Simpson, A. W.	1	0	0
Fletcher, J., Jun., " Wallamumbi "	1	0	0
Cavanagh, J., Guy Faukes	1	0	0

	£	s.	d.
Parke, Major, Guy Faukes	1	0	0
Parry, Robert B.	0	10	6
Baker, F. Mullen, Armidale Road, West Camp	0	10	6
Bray, J., C.P.S., J.P.	0	10	0
Johnstone, Rev. T.	0	10	0
Sheldon, Dr.	0	10	0
Orridge, J.W., J.P.	0	10	0
Scholes, J., Sen.	0	10	0
Scholes, J., Jun.	0	10	0
Gallagher, E.	0	10	0
Davies, D. G.	0	10	0
Wigan, Dr. G.	0	10	0
Scarr, Percy	0	10	0
Day, E.	0	10	0
Jackes, F., J.P.	0	10	0
Craigie and Hipgrave	0	10	0
Buchan, S., "Nymbydia"	0	10	0
Douglass, Miss	0	7	6
Bliss, J.	0	5	0
Cavanagh, A. J.	0	5	0
Drew, W.	0	5	0
Beveridge, A. K.	0	5	0
Stevens, W. H.	0	5	0
Drew, R.	0	5	0
Robberds, Mrs.	0	5	0
Holmes and Apps	0	5	0
Mandel, M.	0	5	0
Allingham, G.	0	5	0
Love, J.	0	5	0

	£	s.	d.
Kirkwood, Mrs.	0	5	0
Hezog, B....	0	5	0
Dunkin, J.	0	5	0
A Friend ...	0	5	0
Cropher, Mrs.	0	5	0
Glass, J. A.	0	5	0
Canning, W.	0	5	0
Sums under 5s.	0	7	0

BENDEMEER.

	£	s.	d.
Scholes, R. "Tara"	1	1	0
Gibson, G. L. "Langford"	1	0	0
Avery, W....	1	0	0
Glover, J. ...	0	10	0
Dixon, J. ...	0	10	0
Edwards, Mrs. ...	0	5	0
Southward, J. ...	0	5	0
McGinty, A.	0	5	0
Parsons, F.	0	5	0
Elbra, W. ...	0	5	0
Dixon, R. G.	0	5	0
Sums under 5s.	0	2	0

BRANXTON.

	£	s.	d.
Wyndham, J., "Dalwood"	2	0	0
Swanston and Martin	1	1	0
Yeomans, R. G., "Belford"	1	1	0
Drynan, Mrs. ...	1	0	0
Wyndham, G., "Fernhill"	1	0	0
Wyndham, R., "Leconfield"	1	0	0
Kelman, J., "Kirkton"...	1	0	0
Tulloch, J. A. ...	0	10	0
A Friend ...	0	5	0
Sums under 5s...	0	2	6

BROUGHTON CREEK.

	£	s.	d.
Wilson, J. and Co. ...	0	10	0
Hill, P. C.	0	5	0

CAMBAWARRA.

	£	s.	d.
Matthews, S. ...	0	10	0
Richards, T. M.	0	10	0
Frazer, James, J.P. ...	0	7	6
McGregor, R. ...	0	5	0
Shepherd, T.	0	5	0
McKenzie, R. ...	0	5	0
McGrath, W. ...	0	5	0
Gibson, John ...	0	5	0
Bice, T. G., J.P.	0	5	0
Sums under 5s.	0	4	6

CAMPBELLTOWN.

	£	s.	d.
Aikin, Rev. T. V., M.A....	1	1	0
Hurley, J., M.P.	1	1	0
Labatt, H. R., Appin	1	1	0
Reddall, the Misses, "Glen Alpine"	1	0	0
Fowler, W., J.P.	0	10	0
Kidd, J., J.P. ...	0	10	0
Fowler, D.	0	10	0
Mackel, F.	0	5	0
Warby, B.	0	5	0
Payton, J....	0	5	0
Bocking, J.	0	5	0
Stewart, T.	0	5	0
A Friend, Appin	0	5	0
Ross, Alex., J.P., Bulli ...	0	5	0
Turnbull, G., Bulli ...	0	5	0
Fry, H., J.P., Woonona...	0	5	0
Sums under 5s...	0	17	0

CHARCOAL.

	£	s.	d.
Jenkins, W. W., J.P.	1	0	0
Richards, J.	0	5	0
Beaties, Mrs.	0	5	0
Phillips, Miss ...	0	5	0

CLARENCE TOWN.

	£	s.	d.
Holmes, W. H.	1	1	0
Johnston, W., J.P., M.L.A.	1	1	0
Donald, Rev. W. S....	1	1	0
Lowe, W., J.P.	0	10	0
Dark, S. W.	0	10	0
A Friend ...	0	5	0
Stronach, W.	0	5	0
Robards, S. T. ...	0	5	0
A Friend ...	0	5	0

DAPTO.

	£	s.	d.
Brown, J. ...	0	10	0
McRae, D.	0	5	0
Hewitt, W.	0	5	0

DENMAN.

	£	s.	d.
White, E., J.P., Martindale	1	10	0
Bellew, Mrs., "Piercefield"	1	1	0
Bell, A., J.P., "Pickering"	0	10	0
Saunders, J. H.	0	10	0
Ross, G.	0	5	0
Jones, C. ...	0	5	0
Sums under 5s.	0	12	6

DUNGOG.

	£	s.	d.
Mackay, J. K., J.P., "Cangoon"	1	1	0
Wade, John	1	1	0
Gorton, Mrs.	1	0	0

	£	s.	d.
Alison, R. L., J.P.	1	0	0
Hooke, B....	0	10	0
Gibson, J....	0	10	0
Nash, Rev. T.	0	10	0
Mackay, G., J.P.	0	10	0
Abbott, Mrs.	0	10	0
Smith, W. A., J.P.	0	10	0
Walker, J...	0	5	0
Tonks, Mrs.	0	5	0
Ryan, M.	0	5	0
McKinley, Dr....	0	5	0
Smith, C. G., P.M.	0	5	0
Durke, Mrs.	0	5	0
Johnston, Rev. R.	0	5	0
Fry, C.	0	5	0
Thornedyke, Mrs.	0	5	0
Piper, E.	0	5	0
Bruyn, D....	0	5	0
Abbott, J....	0	5	0
Burgess, H.	0	5	0
Wade, Mrs.	0	5	0
Carlton, J., J.P.	0	5	0
Sums under 5s....	0	11	0

GERRINGONG.

	£	s.	d.
Wilson, Rev. R.	1	0	0
Miller, William	1	0	0
Hindmarsh, George... ...	0	10	0
Miller, R., J.P...	0	10	0
Miller, Mrs., sen.	0	10	0
Hindmarsh, William, J.P.	0	5	0
Davis, D. F.	0	5	0
Hindmarsh, F. J.	0	5	0
Sums under 5s...	0	11	6

GLEN INNES.

	£	s.	d.
Dumaresq, Mrs. "Furruck-abad"	2	2	0
Dumaresq, W. A., J.P., do.	2	0	0
Robertson, Robert, R. C., J.P., "Wellington Vale," Dundee	1	1	0
Campbell, John	1	1	0
Lewis, H. and R. A. ...	1	1	0
Egan and Noonen	1	1	0
Lewis, E.	0	10	6
Burridge, S. W.	0	10	0
Clark, J.	0	10	0
Scholes, Dr.	0	10	0
Hill, George	0	10	0
Rogerson, W. C.	0	5	0
Fergusson, W. J.	0	5	0
Cash, F.	0	5	0
Cotton, J. J.	0	5	0

	£	s.	d.
Maund, J. E.	0	5	0
Sully, J. and H.	0	5	0
O'Hara, F.	0	5	0
Munro, J....	0	5	0
Marshall, Mrs....	0	5	0
Cavanagh, T.	0	5	0
Sully, W....	0	5	0
Smith, T.	0	5	0
Long, F. W.	0	5	0
Martin, J. J.P.	0	5	0
Dodd, A. J.	0	5	0
O'Horan, T.	0	5	0
Cadden, W. T...	0	5	0
Loveday, T.	0	5	0
Ashton, S....	0	5	0
Boyd, G.	0	5	0
Robinson, J.	0	5	0
Sums under 5s.	0	14	0
Stibbard, W., Dundee ...	0	5	0
Glen Innes Examiner, Advertisements free... ...			
Ditto *Guardian*, Advertisements free			

GRAFTON.

	£	s.	d.
Statham, E. J....	2	2	0
Bawden, Thomas, M.L.A.	1	1	0
Rudd, T. A.	1	1	0
Dixon, J. S., Norton ...	1	1	0
Ryan, E. M., J.P.	1	1	0
Norrie, F....	1	1	0
Selmon, D. B.	1	1	0
Southion Brothers	1	1	0
Hargrave, E., J.P., "Hernani"	1	0	0
Freeman, W., "Greenwich"	1	0	0
McDougall, A. L., P.M. ...	1	0	0
Smith, Rev. John Leslie, B.A.	1	0	0
Cameron, A.	1	0	0
Purdie, Dr...	0	10	6
Munro, J. H.	0	10	6
Jardine and Tennant ...	0	10	6
Dawson, Rev. James W...	0	10	0
Lewington, E. C.	0	10	0
Drinkwater and Kirby ...	0	10	0
Jacobs, Mr. and Mrs. ...	0	10	0
Davidson, P. R.	0	10	0
Holmstean, J. A.	0	10	0
Henderson and Mansfield	0	10	0
James, J.	0	10	0
Wilkinson, W. M.	0	10	0
Mackay, Rev. J.	0	10	0
Smith, S. S.	0	10	0

	£	s.	d.
Davies, J.	0	10	0
Page, Thomas	0	10	0
Rea, John...	0	10	0
Kinnear, W.	0	10	0
Robertson, W., J.P.... ...	0	10	0
Trollope, F.	0	10	0
Grafton Examiner	0	10	0
Grafton Observer	0	10	0
Jardine, Miss	0	5	0
Cumming, J.	0	5	0
Braham, D.	0	5	0
Chapman, F. W., Mayor...	0	5	0
J. S.	0	5	0
Whitford, H.	0	5	0
Carson, J....	0	5	0
Quirk, T.	0	5	0
Muirhead, R.	0 ·	5	0
Ki Koon	0	5	0
Ross, Mrs.	0	5	0
O'Keeffe, Mrs....	0	5	0
Francis, E.	0	5	0
Valckers, H. A.	0	5	0
White, Mrs.	0	5	0
Hockey, E.	0	5	0
Cooper, J....	0	5	0
Robinson, Mrs.	0	5	0
Booth, H....	0	5	0
Duggan, C.	0	5	0
Miller, Mrs.	0	5	0
Attwater, W.	0	5	0
A Friend	0	5	0
Sums under 5s...	0	7	6
Grafton Argus, advertise-ments free			

GRAFTON SOUTH.

	£	s.	d.
Small, Mrs. W., "Swan Creek"	1	0	0
Small, W., J.P., Ditto ...	1	0	0
Neale, G. W., J.P.	1	0	0
Morrow, F.	1	0	0
Whittingham, H.	0	10	0
Andrews, Mrs. S. J., "Urara"	0	10	0
Beatson, D.	0	7	6
Sykes, H.	0	5	0
Aarons, J....	0	5	0
Lowe, F.	0	5	0
Hawthorne, A....	0	5	0
Neale, T....	0	5	0
Seller, T. T.	0	5	0
Neale, W....	0	5	0
Sampson, E.	0	5	0
Hawthorne, T....	0	5	0

HINTON.

	£	s.	d.
Scott, Walter, J.P., "Wallalong," 1876-77	2	0	0
Gally, W....	1	1	0
Christian, W., J.P.	1	1	0
Pearse, Miss	0	10	0
Mann, Mrs.	0	10	0
Geering, H.	0	10	0
Mayo, Mrs.	0	10	0
Wilson, Mrs.	0	10	0
Junar, J. T.	0	5	0
Sums under 5s...	0	9	0

JAMBEROO.

	£	s.	d.
Dymock, D. L....	0	10	6
Tate, John, jun.	0	5	0
Braham, E.	0	5	0
Stewart, W.	0	5	0
Colley, John	0	5	0
Sums under 5s...	0	5	0
Wilson, John, Albion Park	0	5	0

JERRY'S PLAINS.

	£	s.	d.
Bowman, J. W., "Arrowfields"	0	10	6
York, H.	0	10	0
Smith, Rev. E. Huband ...	0	10	0
Stevenson, Mrs.	0	10	0
Brown, J., "Ellerslie" ...	0	10	0
Ryan, M.	0	5	0
Allcorn, R....	0	5	0
Allcorn, R., Jun.	0	5	0
Huxley, Mrs.	0	5	0
Sums under 5s....	0	6	0

KIAMA.

	£	s.	d.
Adams, Mr. and Mrs. ...	1	0	0
Black, J., J.P....	0	10	6
Robb, James, J.P.	0	10	6
Calley, Hugh	0	10	6
Hindmarsh, Nesbitt, J.P.	0	10	0
Calley, James, J.P.	0	10	0
Petric, J. I.	0	10	0
King, W. C.	0	10	0
Marks, Mrs. S....	0	10	0
Calley, W.	0	10	0
Kendall, Thomas, J.P. ...	0	10	0
Marks, Robert...	0	10	0
Bent, Evelyn, a thank offering	0	6	0
Short, W....	0	5	0
Redford, J.	0	5	0
Waldron, G. R.	0	5	0
Major, S.	0	5	0

	£	s.	d.
Wilmot, J.	0	5	0
Newburn, A. W.	0	5	0
Tyter, J. F.	0	5	0
Lewis, W.	0	5	0
Reid, S.	0	5	0
Weston, J.	0	5	0
Bent, S.	0	5	0
Farraher, T.	0	5	0
Woods, W.	0	5	0
Fredericks, H.	0	5	0
Tate, J.	0	5	0
Geoghegan, W.	0	5	0
Honey, T.	0	5	0
Emery, James	0	5	0
Sums under 5s	0	19	6

LOCHINVAR.

	£	s.	d.
Doyle, J. F. and J.	1	1	0
Terrier, P.	0	10	0
Doyle, J.	0	5	0
Walsh, Rev. C.	0	5	0
Read, C.	0	5	0
Green, P., J.P.	0	5	0

MAITLAND WEST.

	£	s.	d.
Briggs, W.	2	2	0
Rourke, J., 1876-77	2	2	0
Pearse, J., Dunmore House	2	0	0
McDougall, A. W., J.P., "Lorn"	2	0	0
Saunders, J. M.	1	1	0
Fraser, J.	1	1	0
Fullford, S. A.	1	1	0
Cohen, N. D.	1	1	0
Thompson, R. W.	1	1	0
Wolfe and Gorrick	1	1	0
Campbell, R.	1	1	0
Brunker, J. N.	1	1	0
Capper, E. P. and Son	1	1	0
Tucker, Gillies, and Thompson	1	1	0
Employees of the above	1	11	0
Dickson, Mrs., "Bolwarra"	1	0	0
Hart, S.	1	0	0
Pierce, Dr. R. J., J.P.	1	0	0
Blair, R.	1	0	0
Owen and Beckett	1	0	0
Hyndes, R., J.P.	1	0	0
Dunn, Capt., Woodville	1	0	0
Finch, Mrs.	1	0	0
Norman, W. R.	0	10	6
Lane, Rev. George	0	10	6
Chapman, Rev. R.	0	10	6
Fullford, J.	0	10	6

	£	s.	d.
Chapman, Rev. R.	0	10	6
Lee, John, J.P.	0	10	6
Logan, P.	0	10	0
Badgery, H.S., J.P., Mayor	0	10	0
Lipscomb, W. G.	0	10	0
Pearse, J., J.P.	0	10	0
Smyth, G. A.	0	8	0
Arnold, Mrs., and family, "Stradbroke"	0	9	0
Casperson, C. H.	0	5	0
Paskins, H.	0	5	0
Barden and Riber	0	5	0
Wolstenholme, J.	0	5	0
Winter, M.	0	5	0
Mills, W. and T.	0	5	0
Humby and Chamberlain	0	5	0
Nies, H.	0	5	0
Arren, W.	0	5	0
Moore, W. T.	0	5	0
Monro, J. and R.	0	5	0
Sheridan, H. A.	0	5	0
Brewer, T. G.	0	5	0
McDougall, Mrs. C.	0	5	0
Barlow, J.	0	5	0
Moore, Mrs. G.	0	5	0
Young, R. A.	0	5	0
Vindin, Mrs. George	0	5	0
Sawyer, J.	0	5	0
Cracknell, R.	0	5	0
A Friend	0	5	0
Cracknell, W.	0	5	0
Winegardner, W.	0	5	0
Solling, G. F.	0	5	0
Fry, Mrs.	0	5	0
Spridgins, Mrs., Quipolly	0	10	0
Sums under 5s	1	4	0

MAITLAND EAST.

	£	s.	d.
Morriset, E. V., J.P.	1	1	0
MacPherson, Rev. P.	1	1	0
Cullum, A. G.	1	0	0
Clift, S.	1	0	0
Clift, G.	0	10	6
Scholey, S., M.P.	0	10	0
Price, J., "Buttai"	0	10	0
Petherbridge, W.	0	10	0
Jones, J. S.	0	10	0
Tyrrell, Rev. L.	0	10	0
Chambers, G. T.	0	10	0
Muir, Mrs.	0	5	6
Coberoft, A. J.	0	5	6
Brown, R. P.	0	5	0
Willie, J.	0	5	0
Bourke, P.	0	5	0

	£	s.	d
Dewar, H. E.	0	5	0
Garvis, A. E.	0	5	0
Delohery, C., C.P.S... ...	0	5	0
Sums under 5s....	0	1	0

MILTON.

	£	s.	d
Wheatley, Mrs.	1	17	6
Warden, David, J.P.,"Airlie House"	1	1	0
Ewin, W. W., J.P., Woodstock	1	1	0
Hough, Rev. W.	1	0	0
Warden, D., J.P., "Airlie House"...	1	0	0
Seccombe, R.	0	10	6
Kendall, John, J.P.... ...	0	10	0
Kendall, W.	0	10	0
Chapman, William J. ...	0	10	0
Mathison, W.	0	10	0
Griffin, W...	0	5	0
Hayley, W. F.	0	5	0
Blackburn, H. C.	0	5	0
Watts, D.	0	5	0
Mitchell, T.	0	5	0
Mulligan, E. T.	0	5	0
Pickering, S.	0	5	0
McArthur, A.	0	5	0
Wilford, W. H...	0	5	0
Kendall, Walter	0	5	0
Sums under 5s....	0	2	6

MORPETH.

	£	s.	d
Eales, John, "Duckenfield"	5	0	0
Bettington, J. B., J.P. "Brindley Park," Merriwa	3	3	0
Child, Rev. Canon	1	1	0
Dargin, J. W.	1	0	0
Nainby, F.	0	10	6
Sim, D., Mayor	0	10	0
Dye, Capt., J.P.	0	10	0
Moffitt, R.	0	10	0
Meiklejohn, J.	0	10	0
Geary, H....	0	10	0
Haydon, P. K....	0	7	6
Lee, J. W.	0	7	6
Moffitt, T....	0	5	0
Wilson, C.	0	5	0
Wakely, C. F.	0	5	0
Blake, W....	0	5	0
Nixon, Mrs.	0	5	0
Lowry, W.	0	5	0
Kite, G.	0	5	0
Sums under 5s...	0	13	6

MURRURUNDI.

	£	s.	d.
Wright, P. W., J.P., "Bickham"	2	0	0
Abbott, J. P.	1	1	0
Abbott, Mrs., "Glengarry"	1	1	0
Jaques, W. F.	1	1	0
Tebbutt, T. L....	1	1	0
Knowles, Dr. W. B... ...	1	0	0
Potts, W. E.	1	0	0
Maclain, A.	1	0	0
Gamble, G.	1	0	0
Ross, Rev. J.	0	10	6
Brodie, G. G., J.P. ...	0	10	6
Brodie, A., J.P. ...	0	10	6
Guest, T.	0	10	6
Street, C. B.	0	10	0
Perry, T. B. and Co. ...	0	10	0
Grehan, Brothers	0	10	0
Puckley, T. F. G.	0	10	0
Denshire, J.	0	10	0
Phillips and Munro... ...	0	10	0
Johnston, T. A., J.P., "Hartfell" Gunnadah, ...	0	10	0
Selden, W. F.	0	10	0
Kingsmill, A. J., J.P. ...	0	5	6
Ingall, R.	0	5	0
Kickham, J.	0	5	0
Bransfield, J.	0	5	0
Guest, W. C.	0	5	0
Long, W.	0	5	0
Cox, F. W.	0	5	0
Nicholl, W.	0	5	0
Harrison, J.	0	5	0
Arnott, J. S.	0	5	0
Long, W.	0	5	0
Haydon, Mrs., "Bloomfield"	0	5	0
Whiteman, Mrs., Sen., ditto	0	5	0
Whiteman, Mrs. A., ditto	0	5	0
Sums under 5s....	0	11	0

MUSWELLBROOK.

	£	s.	d.
Blunt, G.	2	2	0
White, Mrs., sen.	2	0	0
White, Rev. Canon... ...	1	1	0
Campbell, M.	1	1	0
Doyle, J. F., "Dartmouth"	1	1	0
Cox, J. H., "Negoa" ...	1	0	0
Keys, J. H., J.P., "Bengalla"	1	0	0
Nowland, A., "Overton"	1	0	0
Hall, Mrs., Dartbrook ...	1	0	0
Hall, Miss, ditto	1	0	0
Wilson, Rev. W. S., Cassilis	1	0	0

	£	s.	d.
Doyle, J. F., jun., J.P., "Rosebrook"	0	10	6
Grigson, Dr. R. E.	0	10	6
Luscombe, R. J.	0	10	0
Evans, D.	0	10	0
Mitchell, A. J.	0	10	0
Eaton, Mrs.	0	10	0
Laing, Rev. J. S.	0	7	0
Foley, T., C.P.S.	0	5	0
Hodges, W.	0	5	0
Clark, A.	0	5	0
Green, Mrs. S.	0	5	0
Flower, G.	0	5	0
Whitehead, Mrs.	0	5	0
Dowell, S. J.	0	5	0
Denshire, W. C.	0	5	0
Parkinson, J.	0	5	0
Sawkins, C. E.	0	5	0
Sums under 5s	0	16	6

NEWCASTLE.

	£	s.	d.
Merewether, Mrs., "The Ridge"	3	3	0
Innis, T.	2	2	0
Selwyn, Rev. Canon, 1876–1877	2	0	0
Knaggs, R. C. and Co.	1	1	0
Wood Brothers	1	1	0
Dibbs, J. C.	1	1	0
Ash, F.	1	1	0
Wallace, R. B., J.P.	1	1	0
Ellis, J. C.	1	1	0
Brown, J. and A.	1	1	0
Hobbs, W. J.	1	1	0
Finch, H.	1	1	0
Innes, Thomas	1	1	0
Wallace, George, Mayor	1	1	0
Lockhead, W. K.	1	0	0
Harris, R.	1	0	0
Mitchell, G.	1	0	0
Slater, T. B.	1	0	0
Ireland, J.	1	0	0
Millar, Mrs. D.	1	0	0
Bode, Rev. F. D.	1	0	0
Ash, J.	1	0	0
Hewison, G., J.P.	1	0	0
Bolton, Major	1	0	0
Martin, J.	1	0	0
Lister, M.	1	0	0
Knaggs, Mrs. S. T.	0	15	6
Rowe, W. W.	0	10	6
Capper, W. C. H.	0	10	6
Spence, B.	0	10	6
H. B. C.	0	10	0

	£	s.	d.
Sweetland, C.	0	10	0
Jewell, W. M.	0	10	0
Robson, W., J.P.	0	10	0
Pepper, J.	0	10	0
Ludlow, Mrs.	0	10	0
A Friend	0	10	0
Pepper, Rev. T. J.	0	10	0
Brown, H. J.	0	10	0
Russell, J.	0	10	0
Tudor, T.	0	10	0
Kittson, J. J.	0	10	0
Clack, T. A.	0	10	0
Cloudy, Mrs.	0	10	0
Sparke, W. A.	0	10	0
Dixon, W.	0	5	0
Watt, Alex.	0	5	0
Sayer, W.	0	5	0
Allen, Captain	0	5	0
Gardner, F.	0	5	0
O'Gallaher, E.	0	5	0
Bonarius, J. C.	0	5	0
Watt, Mrs.	0	5	0
Arnott, W.	0	5	0
Beckenridge, K.	0	5	0
Asher, A.	0	5	0
Baker, W. H.	0	5	0
Macdermott, F. S. & Co	0	5	0
Herald, E.	0	5	0
Coutts, Rev. J.	0	5	0
Rogers, J. S.	0	5	0
Fleming, R.	0	5	0
Higgs, J.	0	5	0
Chippendall, E., Jun.	0	5	0
Pallister, G.	0	5	0
Sums under 5 shillings	0	19	6
Tighe, A. A. P., P.M., Waratah	1	1	0
Moody, Mrs., Waratah	0	10	0
Watson, D., ditto	0	10	0
Hill, J. J., J.P., Lambton	1	1	0
Proprietors of *Newcastle Pilot*, advertisements free			

PATERSON.

	£	s.	d.
Corner, W., J.P.	1	0	0
A Friend, "Tocal"	0	10	0
Addams, Rev. F. W.	0	10	0
Newbury, Dr.	0	10	0
McCormach, J., J.P.	0	10	0
Cann, J.	0	5	0
Cann, F. W.	0	5	0
Smith, J. G.	0	5	0
Puxty, Mrs.	0	5	0
Riekie, D.	0	5	0

	£	s.	d.
Keppie, W.	0	5	0
Sums under 5s....	0	4	6

QUEANBEYAN.
Collected by W. G. O'Neill.

	£	s.	d.
Ware, Rev. J. M.	1	1	0
Russell, Col., P.M.	1	1	0
Rutledge, Thomas, J.P. ...	1	1	0
Cunningham, A., J.P. ...	1	1	0
Ryrie, A., J.P.	1	1	0
Ryrie, Mrs. A.	1	1	0
Morton, Dr., J.P.	1	0	0
Harcourt, G.	1	0	0
Cunningham, A. J., J.P. ...	1	0	0
Nugent, J. W.	1	0	0
Davis, Wm., J.P.	1	0	0
Church of England collections	1	0	0
H.H.L. Oddfellows, M.U.	1	0	0
McKellar, R. W.	0	10	6
O'Neill, W. G.	0	10	6
Mehegan, R.	0	10	6
Doonan, J.	0	10	6
Williams, O., C.P.S. ...	0	10	0
Whiteside, E. T.	0	10	0
Naylor, Peter	0	10	0
McNamara, J., London bridge	0	10	0
Heslop, J.	0	10	0
McKeahnie, Charles ...	0	10	0
Cameron, K.	0	10	0
Gabriel, A. W.	0	5	0
Gifford, G., Jun.	0	5	0
Marshall, J.	0	5	0
Parr, Thos., Solicitor ...	0	5	0
Hollett, Wm.	0	5	0
Brown, James	0	5	0
Spratt, J. B.	0	5	0
Hunt, Wm.	0	5	0
Land, Edwin	0	5	0
Cane, Henry	0	5	0
Laing, T. J.	0	5	0
Laing, Master T. H... ...	0	5	0
Cane, Miss M. A.	0	5	0
Doonan, Miss	0	5	0
Scott, Miss Kate	0	5	0
Jones, C. J.	0	5	0
Kealman, J.	0	5	0
Van Heythuysen, R. ...	0	5	0
Myers, A.	0	5	0
Taylor, Rev. J. G.	0	5	0
Buttle, Thomas	0	5	0
Willans, O. A.	0	5	0

	£	s.	d.
Jacob, V.	0	5	0
McKeahnie, N.	0	5	0
Wilson, Thomas	0	5	0
Palmer, P. C.	0	5	0
Sums under 5s...	5	16	6

QUIRINDI.

	£	s.	d.
Underwood, E., J.P., Mrs. Underwood ..:	2	10	0
Tabbutt, J. W....	0	10	0
Allen, R. A.	0	5	0
O'Neile, H.	0	5	0
Salomons, H. B.	0	5	0
Cook, B.	0	5	0
Sums under 5s...	0	7	6

RAYMOND TERRACE.

	£	s.	d.
Windeyer, J., J.P., "Kinross"	2	0	0
A Friend	0	10	0
Simm, Rev. S.	0	10	0
Shaw, W. E.	0	10	0
Windeyer, Mrs. T. A. ...	0	10	0
Keene, Mrs.	0	10	0
Kent, W.	0	10	0
Hart, J. S.	0	10	0
Richardson and Scully ...	0	5	0
Kent, Mrs. W.	0	5	0
Campbell, D. J.	0	5	0
Sums under 5s...	0	2	6
Carmichael, G. T. and J. B., Seaham	1	0	0
Fisher, W., Seaham... ...	0	10	0

SCONE. .

	£	s.	d.
Vernon, J.	3	3	0
Cook, T., "Turanville" ...	2	2	0
Bolding, H. J....	1	1	0
Creed, Dr., J.P.	1	0	0
Little, J.	1	0	0
Broughton, E.	1	0	0
Miller, M....	1	0	0
Garrett, J. P.M.	1	0	0
Brown, F., "St. Aubins"	0	10	0
Ayling, Rev. J.	0	10	0
Isaac, F.	0	10	0
Evans, Mrs.	0	10	0
Johnston, A.	0	10	0
Nicholl, Mrs.	0	10	0
Asser, N. F.	0	10	0
Goodwin, Mrs....	0	10	0
Ferguson, R.	0	10	0
Campbell, D.	0	5	6
McLaughlin, W.	0	5	0

	£	s.	d.
Terry, J.	0	5	0
Hayne, F....	0	5	0
Hannabus, J.	0	5	0
Hopper, G.	0	5	0
A Friend	0	5	0
Tinch, E. J., "Clifdale"	0	5	0
Sums under 5s.	0	9	6

SHELLHARBOUR.

	£	s.	d.
Dunster, W. and H. ...	0	10	0
Dunster, J., J.P.	0	10	0
Coughran, Mrs.	0	5	0
Barrs, Miss	0	5	0
Allen, Mrs.	0	5	0
Hall, Richard	0	5	0
Sums under 5s...	0	11	6

SHOALHAVEN.

	£	s.	d.
Berry, David, "Coolangatta," 1874-75	2	0	0
Berry, David, "Coolangatta," 1876-77	2	2	0
Hyam, M., J.P., Nowra...	1	1	0
Ratnell, W., per M. Hyam, Esq., J.P. ...	1	1	0
Morton, H. G....	1	0	0
Lovegrove, W., C.P.S., Nowra	0	15	0
McArthur, J. and Co. ...	0	10	6
Phillips, Rev. J.	0	10	0
Brettell, C. C., "Coolangatta"	0	10	0
Graham, James	0	10	0
Armstrong, James	0	5	0
Pooley, E....	0	5	0
Flatt, T. W., Commercial Bank, Terrara	0	5	0
Weller, John	0	5	0
Brown, M.	0	5	0
Moss, Henry, Nowra ...	0	5	0
Green, J.	0	5	0
Hyam, D., Terrara	0	5	0
Sums under 5s....	0	17	0

SINGLETON.

	£	s.	d.
Howe, J. K., "Redburnbury" 1876-7	4	4	0
Dangar, A. A., "Baroona"	3	3	0
Dangar, W. J., "Neatsfield"	2	2	0
Loder, G., "Abbey Green"	2	2	0
Ravensworth Estate ...	2	2	0
Brown, John	2	2	0

	£	s.	d.
Munro, A.	2	0	0
McKenzie, W., and Employees at A. Munro, Esq.	1	6	6
Howe, Mrs., per Mrs. John Hay	1	1	0
Loder, Capt. T. G., J.P., Wylie's Flat...	1	1	0
Ash, W.	1	1	0
Campbell, J. W.	1	1	0
Glennie, H., J.P.	1	1	0
Jay, R. F....	1	1	0
Moore, J....	1	0	0
Dixon, E.	1	1	0
Bowman, Alex.	1	1	0
Hooke, Aug., J.P., Hamilton Hill	1	1	0
Brown, Mrs. J. H.	1	1	0
Durham, J., 1876-77 ...	1	1	0
McDouall, J. C., J.P., "New Freujh"	1	0	0
Horne, S. H.	1	0	0
Hartley, R. B., (Young and Lark)	1	0	0
Dight, Mrs. E. M. "Stafford"	1	0	0
Dight, S. B., J.P., "Clifford"	1	0	0
McKay, D. F.	1	0	0
Jarman, G., J.P.	0	10	6
McFadden, H....	0	10	6
Dalton, R.	0	10	0
Shaw, Rev. B. C., B.A. ...	0	10	0
Dudding, W., J.P., C.P.S.	0	10	0
Larnach, J. A....	0	10	0
Read, Dr. R.	0	10	0
Hutchinson, J.	0	10	0
Waddy, Percy	0	10	0
Belfrage, G. H. E.	0	10	0
Gould, A. J.	0	10	0
Waddell, W., Sen.	0	10	0
Morrison, D.	0	10	0
Wilson, S.	0	5	0
Gardiner, F. W.	0	5	0
Quinn, J. Patrick	0	5	0
Lawkins, E. B....	0	5	0
Upjohn, O. R.	0	5	0
Ham, E.	0	5	0
Christian, J.	0	5	0
Kelf, J.	0	5	0
Spink, Mrs.	0	5	0
Ellis, Thomas	0	5	0
Jackson, T.	0	5	0
Faucett, Mrs.	0	5	0

	£	s.	d.
Johnston, Mrs....	0	5	0
Munro, Hugh	0	5	0
Clerehew, W.	0	5	0
Broomfield, ——	0	5	0
Dight, S. B., Jun.	0	5	0
Sums under 5s.	0	13	0

TAMWORTH.

	£	s.	d.
Gill, John, J.P., Moonby	1	1	0
Gill, G. R., J.P., ditto ...	1	1	0
Stewart, Seymour C. ...	1	1	0
Lewis, Brothers	1	1	0
Irwin, D. W., P.M.... ...	1	1	0
Lambert, J.	1	1	0
Hudson, R., " Warrah "...	1	1	0
Cohen and Levy	1	1	0
Lambert, S.	1	1	0
Cooper, E....	1	0	0
Gay, E.	0	10	0
Goodwin, D. R...	0	10	0
Callaghan, J.	0	10	0
Blackall and Co.	0	10	0
Tribe and Newman	0	10	0
Allen, W.	0	10	0
Garland, J., J.P.	0	10	0
Aiken, Brothers	0	10	0
Godson, T. A.	0	10	0
Gosling and Smart	0	10	0
Hughes, F.	0	10	0
Cohen, N. and Co. ...	0	10	0
Patter-on, J.	0	10	0
Vett Her Von	0	10	0
King, T.	0	5	0
Settatree, Mrs....	0	5	0
Turton, T. P.	0	5	0
Nancarrow, J.	0	5	0
Throsby, W.	0	5	0
Denning and Barden ...	0	5	0
Grayston, T.	0	5	0
Jenne, L. C.	0	5	0
Smith, C.	0	5	0
Blake, P.	0	5	0
Dowe, Mrs.	0	5	0
French, G. F.	0	5	0
Partens, J. A.	0	5	0
Sinclair, Mrs.	0	5	0
Bedwell, C. W...	0	5	0
Madden, A.	0	5	0
Little, R.	0	5	0
Little, Mrs. A. E.	0	5	0
McNaught, A.	0	5	0
Beckett, T. S.	0	5	0

TENTERFIELD.

	£	s.	d.
Irby, E., J.P., " Bolivia "	2	2	0
Lee, Charles A., J.P., 1876-7	2	2	0
Drummond, W.	1	1	0
Cavanaugh, C. I.	1	1	0
Peberdy, T., Mayor... ...	1	1	0
O'Connell, E.	1	1	0
Brown, J. J.	1	1	0
Whereat, E. R., J.P. ...	1	1	0
Simpson, J. M., Tenterfield Station	1	1	0
Bernstein, Dr.	0	10	6
Carr, E. P.	0	10	6
Hennessey, Rev. John D.	0	10	6
Graham, J. B., P.M. ...	0	10	6
Lockhart, W. S.	0	10	0
Addison, J. F....	0	10	0
O'Connell, Mrs.	0	10	0
Tindale, G. H....	0	7	6
Young, W.	0	5	0
Keeve, J. D.	0	5	0
A Friend	0	5	0
Krake, L.	0	5	0
Simons, J., C.P.S.	0	5	0
Lenihan, Sin See	0	5	0
Laird, W....	0	5	0
Graham, A. W.	0	5	0
Pavel, C.	0	5	0
Sums under 5s., per Mrs. J. J. Brown	0	15	0

ULLADULLA.

	£	s.	d.
Sturrock, W.	1	0	0
Millard, W. and G.... ...	0	10	0
Cashman, W.	0	10	0
Fitch, C.	0	5	0
Seccombe, E.	0	5	0
McKenzie, R.	0	5	0

ULMARRA.

	£	s.	d.
Small, Mrs. T....	1	0	0
Pateman, John	1	0	0
See, S.	1	0	0
Cameron, Alexander, J.P., Rockymouth...	1	0	0
Browne, T.	0	10	0
Clark, T.	0	10	0
Napper, E.	0	10	0
Quale, W....	0	10	0
McDougall, Miss	0	10	0
Miller, J.	0	10	0
Amos, W....	0	10	0
McFarlane, Mrs.	0	6	0
Thornton, George	0	5	0

	£	s.	d.
Granger, John...	0	5	0
Granger, W. A.	0	5	0
James, J. M.	0	5	0
Gruer, Mrs.	0	5	0
McMillan, J.	0	5	0
Lee, T.	0	5	0
Kelly, Mrs.	0	5	0
Lee, W.	0	5	0
Young, Mrs.	0	5	0
Doyle, Miss	0	5	0
Miller, J., jun....	0	5	0
Miller, Hugh	0	5	0
McLoud, A.	0	5	0
Sums under 5s...	0	5	6
Hopkins, Rev. J., Brushgrove	0	10	0
Anderson, D., Brushgrove	0	10	0

URALLA.

	£	s.	d.
White, Fred. R., J.P., "Rookwood," 1876-77...	2	0	0
Sinclair, Rev. D. M., C. E.	1	0	0
Conally, W. H.	0	10	0
McCrossin, J.	0	10	0
Haines, J....	0	5	0
Carroll, J....	0	5	0
Falconer, J.	0	5	0
Purkiss, H.	0	5	0
McCrossin, W. S.	0	5	0
Jones, W. A.	0	5	0
Robke, H....	0	5	0
Sums under 5s....	0	9	0
Uralla and Walcha *Times* advertisements free			

WALCHA.

	£	s.	d.
Nevison, A., J.P., "Ohio"	2	0	0
Daniel, Mrs. J.	1	1	0
Hardaker, T. O.	1	1	0
Marsh, Mrs., "Salisbury Court" ...	1	1	0
Taylor, Mrs., "Terrible Vale" ...	1	1	0
Scott, Mrs., "Surveyors Creek"...	1	0	0
Nevison, J. A., "Ohio"...	1	0	0
Airey, Charles B., C.P.S...	0	10	0
Erratt, G. H., J.P....	0	10	0
Walsh, M. J. ...	0	10	0
Hamilton, J.	0	10	0
Johnston, J.	0	10	0
Mitchell, A.	0	10	0
Robinson, Rev. C. G.	0	5	0
Bath, T.	0	5	0
Studdy, A. H. ...	0	5	0
Farrell, S....	0	5	0

WALLABADAH.

	£	s.	d.
Macdonald, J. M. L., J.P., "Wallabadah" ...	1	1	0
Davies, Dr. J. W. ...	1	1	0
Dight, Mrs. C. H., "Goonoo Goonoo" ...	1	0	0
King, G. B. G., "Goonoo Goonoo" ...	0	10	0
Dettmer, E. C....	0	5	0
Bogan, E....	0	5	0
Berry, Mrs.	0	5	0
Kelly, A. ...	0	5	0
Hogan, D. J.	0	5	0
Turner, W.	0	5	0
Cropper, Mrs., Deep Creek	0	5	0
Sums under 5s...	0	8	6

WOLLONGONG.

	£	s.	d.
Osborne, James	1	1	0
Bright, J.	1	1	0
Cox, Mrs. ...	0	10	0
Turner, A. A., P.M...	0	10	0
Wilson, R.	0	10	0
Woodward, F. ...	0	10	0
Osborne, Mrs. W. ...	0	10	0
Lyons, Dr..	0	10	0
Barton, Mrs.	0	10	0
Brown, Rev. J. W. ...	0	10	0
Cole, F. R.	0	10	0
Campbell and Hart...	0	10	0
Robertson, W. G.	0	10	0
Davis, Mrs.	0	10	0
A Friend ...	0	5	0
Hoskins, J. W....	0	5	0
McDonald, D. ...	0	5	0
Brown, C....	0	5	0
Jones, E. A.	0	5	0
Parsons, A.	0	5	0
Parsons, R.	0	5	0
Wilmot, J.	0	5	0
Beatson, A.	0	5	0
Collins, T., Mayor ...	0	5	0
Sievert, H. C. F.	0	5	0
Stewart, Rev. J. A....	0	5	0
Ponder, J....	0	5	0
Griffin, D., Sen.	0	5	0
Griffin, D., Jun.	0	5	0
Young, J....	0	5	0
Edmonds, W. ...	0	5	0
Wiseman, W. J.	0	5	0
Graham, A.	0	5	0
Comens, G. W...	0	5	0
Bow, Mrs....	0	5	0
Sums under 5s....	1	3	0

QUEENSLAND.

ALLORA.

	£	s.	d.
Clark, C., J.P., "East Talgai"	£2	0	0
Campbell, Rev. H. J. ...	0	10	0
Kates, T., J.P., Mayor ...	0	10	0
Gordon, S.	0	5	0
Kennedy, T.	0	5	0
Burge, W.	0	5	0
Cranitch, P.	0	5	0
Deacon, W.	0	5	0
Cook, R....	0	5	0

BRISBANE.

	£	s.	d.
His Excellency Sir Arthur E. Kennedy, K.C.M.G., C.B.	5	0	0
Palmer, Hon. A. H., M.L.A.	3	3	0
Douglas, Hon. J., M.L.A.	2	2	0
Griffith, Hon. S. W., M.L.A.	2	2	0
Mein, Hon. C. S., M.L.A.	2	2	0
Right Rev. Lord Bishop of Brisbane	2	2	0
Lilley, Mr. Justice	2	2	0
Walsh, W. H., M.L.A. ...	2	2	0
Morehead, B. D., M.L.A.	2	2	0
Beor, H. R., M.L.A. ...	2	2	0
Bramston, H., J.P.... ...	2	2	0
Stewart, A., J.P.	2	2	0
Raff, A., J.P.	2	2	0
Raff, G. and Co.	2	2	0
Brown, D. L. and Co. ...	2	2	0
Butler, W., "Kilcoy" ...	2	2	0
Edmondstone, Hon. G., M.L.C.	2	0	0
Brown, Hon. A. H., M.L.C.	2	0	0
Abbott, H. P., J.P.... ..	2	0	0
King, Hon. H. E., M.L.A.	1	1	0
Gregory, A. C., C.M.G. ...	1	1	0
Thornton, Hon. W., M.L.C.	1	1	0
Simpson, Hon. Captain, M.L.C.	1	1	0
Hobbs, Hon. W., M.L.C.	1	1	0
Stewart, R. M., M.L.A. ...	1	1	0
Miles, Hon. W., M.L.A.	1	1	0
Dickson, Hon. J. R., M.L.A.	1	1	0

	£	s.	d.
Thorne, Hon. G., M.L.A.	1	1	0
Fraser, S., M.L.A.	1	1	0
Murphy, W. E., M.L.A....	1	1	0
Byerley, F. J., J.P.... ...	1	1	0
Whish, Captain, J.P. ...	1	1	0
Heath, Captain, R.N. ...	1	1	0
Wyborn, Captain	1	1	0
Martin, Arthur, J.P. ...	1	1	0
Lukin, G. L., J.P.	1	1	0
Jones, Rev. T.	1	1	0
Beattie, F., M.L.A.... ...	1	1	0
Quinlan, M., J.P.	1	1	0
Barnett, E. and Co. ...	1	1	0
Street, Edward	1	1	0
Mort, Holland, and Co. ...	1	1	0
Webster and Co.	1	1	0
Edwards and Chapman ...	1	1	0
Macpherson, P.	1	1	0
Taylor, W. S.	1	1	0
Potts, Paul, and Sargant...	1	1	0
Sinclair, D.	1	1	0
Stanley, H. C.	1	1	0
Little and Browne	1	1	0
Williams, W.	1	1	0
Baynes, W.	1	1	0
Shaw, Alfred, and Co. ...	1	1	0
Brown, W. J.	1	1	0
Thompson, A., J.P.... ...	1	1	0
Thompson and Hellicar ...	1	1	0
Chambers, A. W.	1	1	0
Brabant and Co.	1	1	0
Wakefield, H.	1	1	0
Jacobs, J. and Co.	1	1	0
Herbert, A. O., J.P... ...	1	0	0
Tully, W. A., J.P.	1	0	0
Petrie, J., J.P....	1	0	0
Drury, E. R., J.P.	1	0	0
Emmelhainz, Dr.	1	0	0
Roe, R. H., M.A.	1	0	0
Honeyman, J.	1	0	0
Kennedy and de Fraine ...	1	0	0
Oxley, H. J.	1	0	0
A. A....	1	0	0
W. P....	1	0	0
Phillips, P...	1	0	0
Carmichael, L....	1	0	0

	£	s.	d.		£	s.	d.
Fletcher, C.	1	0	0	Callaghan, J.	0	10	0
Huntley, G.	1	0	0	Donald, R.	0	10	0
Cameron, J., J.P.	0	10	6	Roche, F. W.	0	10	0
Armour, R., J.P.	0	10	6	Merrett, F.	0	10	0
Ward, M., J.P.	0	10	6	Enright, C. H....	0	10	0
Armour, R. L....	0	10	6	Gibson, Mrs.	0	10	0
Butler Brothers	0	10	6	Mahalm, Rev. R.	0	10	0
Widdop, W.	0	10	6	Jessop, J. S.	0	10	0
Berkley and Taylor... ...	0	10	6	R. S. S.	0	5	0
F. R....	0	10	6	J. F. N. P.	0	5	0
Ellis, J. B., and Co.... ...	0	10	6	Adam, R. D.	0	5	0
Finney, T., J.P....	0	10	0	Carsens, T. D. A.	0	5	0
E. B....	0	10	0	Wurk, S.	0	5	0
E. D....	0	10	0	Hall, W.	0	5	0
Baldwin, C.	0	10	0	Conroy, J....	0	5	0
Munro, C....	0	10	0	Harris, M	0	5	0
Grimley, S	0	10	0	Black, J. M.	0	5	0
Barker, A. J.	0	10	0	Eldridge, F.	0	5	0
Potts, J.	0	10	0	Sums under 5s...	0	10	0
Griffith, Rev. E.	0	10	0	Macmichael, J. T., "Con-			
Sutton, J. W.	0	10	0	damine Plains "	1	1	0
Munce, W. J.	0	10	0	Morrison, R., ditto... ...	0	10	0
M'Nab, D.	0	10	0	McEwan, W., ditto.. ...	0	10	0
Watson and Ferguson ...	0	10	0	Mills, W., ditto... ...	0	2	6
Costin, T. A.	0	10	0	Walker, S., ditto... ...	0	2	0
Aitchison, W.	0	10	0	Evans, A. H., " St. Ruth "	1	0	0
Lukin, G.	0	10	0	Newdick, F. S., ditto ...	0	10	0
Hill, Walter	0	10	0	Davie, S. ditto ...	0	5	0
M'Naught, J. U.	0	10	0	Corry, Mrs., "Cecil Plains"	1	0	0
Smith, E., Edward-street...	0	10	0	Boulton, G., ditto ...	0	10	0
F. C.	0	5	0	Brodribb and Co., " Kur-			
A Friend	0	5	0	rowah "...	1	1	0
Chancellar, W....	0	5	0				
Moxley, T. C.	0	5	0	**FELTON STATION.**			
A Friend	0	5	0				
E. B. C.	0	5	0	Tyson, J., J.P....	5	5	0
Keith, W....	0	5	0	Donely and Hewitt	2	0	0
Snow, C. W.	0	5	0	Whitchurch	0	10	6
Sums under 5s....	1	3	6	Horn, W....	0	5	0
Per favor of G. D. Harrison—				O'Keefe, P.	0	5	0
Stephens, Hon.T.B.,M.L.C.	1	1	0	Tighe, P.	0	5	0
Wassell	1	1	0	Kane, J.	0	5	0
Harrison, G. D...	0	10	6	Watson, Mrs., Felton Hotel	0	5	0
W. H. H....	0	2	6	**GOWRIE STATION.**			
DALBY.				King, G., J.P.	2	2	0
				King, G. B., J.P.	1	1	0
Robertson, Rev. P.	1	0	0	King, H. V.	1	1	0
Jordan, M.	0	10	6				
Yaldwin, W., P.M.... ...	0	10	0	**IPSWICH.**			
R. T. S.	0	10	0	Cribb and Foote	5	5	0
Dunn, S.	0	10	0	Von Lossberg, Dr., J.P. ...	2	0	0
O'Brien, D.	0	10	0	Ivory, J.	1	1	0
Mohoupt, H.	0	10	0	Cameron, D.	1	1	0
				Hughes and Cameron ...	1	1	0

	£	s.	d.
Cannan, J. K.	1	1	0
Wilson, G. A. and Co. ...	1	1	0
Reilly, J.	1	1	0
Fallon, R., J.P...	1	1	0
Proprietors of the Ipswich *Observer*	1	1	0
McDonald, Mrs., "Dungandan"	1	1	0
Meyer and Isambert ...	1	0	0
Daisey, M.	1	0	0
Kingsmill, H. C.	1	0	0
Gaggs, M., Goodna	1	0	0
Proprietors of the Queensland *Times*	0	15	0
Towely, Capt., P.M... ...	0	10	6
Browne, Rev. F. H.... ...	0	10	6
Shenton, S., J.P.	0	10	6
Wilson, Mrs. G. A.	0	10	6
Wilson, G. R.	0	10	6
Cribb, T. B.	0	10	6
Whitehouse, F...	0	10	6
North, Rev. Roger	0	10	0
Weise, G. R.	0	10	0
Johnston, Mrs. J.	0	10	0
Gibson, J....	0	10	0
Thompson, Mrs.	0	10	0
Kennedy, Dr.	0	10	0
Macfarlane and Son... ...	0	10	0
Cameron, Gordon	0	10	0
Henderson, Mrs. J.... ...	0	10	0
Wright, R.	0	10	0
Brentnall, Rev. F. T. ...	0	10	0
Sweeney, P.	0	10	0
Hutchinson, A. M., J.P....	0	10	0
Francis, J.	0	10	0
Hoey, T. W.	0	10	0
A Friend	0	10	0
O'Sullivan, J.	0	10	0
Gill, R.	0	10	0
Vowles, W.	0	10	0
Lyon, T. B.	0	10	0
A Friend	0	9	0
Barr, Mrs...	0	7	6
McGrath, J.	0	7	6
Brady, T. W.	0	7	6
Challinor, G. M.	0	5	0
A Friend	0	5	0
Roderick, T.	0	5	0
Baines, E.	0	5	0
H. B. B.	0	5	0
O'Malley, M., C.P.S. ...	0	5	0
McGill, J....	0	5	0
W. H.	0	5	0

	£	s.	d.
Real, M.	0	5	0
Southwood, Mrs.	0	5	0
Scott, J.	0	5	0
Tutham, W.	0	5	0
Shanks, H.	0	5	0
McDonald A.	0	5	0
Gorry, C., J.P....	0	5	0
Powell, F....	0	5	0
Hockley, J.	0	5	0
Kendall, R. J....	0	5	0
S. S.	0	5	0
Bowers, M.	0	5	0
Henderson, W...	0	5	0
Henderson, R....	0	5	0
Halley, J....	0	5	0
Towell, T....	0	5	0
Foote, Alfred M.	0	5	0
Brown, W.	0	5	0
Ware, G.	0	5	0
Harrap, G.	0	5	0
North, J.	0	5	0
Zillman, Rev. M.	0	5	0
Buldrey, C.	0	5	0
Meredith, Mrs....	0	5	0
Fleischmann, I. F.	0	5	0
Sums under 5s.	1	1	6

JONDARYAN STATION.

	£	s.	d.
Cock, S.	1	0	0
Mirchinn, F.	1	0	0
Miers, J.	0	10	0
Schell, J.	0	10	0
Mason, W...	0	10	0
Tully, Margaret	0	10	0
Evans, T.	0	10	0
Hodgson, W.	0	5	0
Hodgson, G.	0	5	0
Galwan, E.	0	5	0
Flanagan, D.	0	5	0
Robinson, W.	0	5	0
Arnold, F....	0	5	0
Haywood, J.	0	2	6
Goll, J., Jondaryan Railway Station	0	5	0
"Do EverGood," Jondaryan Hotel	2	2	0

LEYBURN.

	£	s.	d.
Hogarth, W., "Balgownie"	2	0	0
Hanmer, Mrs. "Talgai"	1	1	0
Bracker, H., J.P., "Warroo"	1	0	0
Snell, J., J.P., "Ellengowan"...	1	0	0

	£	s.	d.		£	s.	d.
Kirby, Mrs.	0	5	0	Glanville, G. W.	0	10	0
Boeddner, F.	0	5	0	Pearson, J. A.	0	10	0
Kennedy, D.	0	5	0	McLeith and Waugh ...	0	10	0
Lea, W. J.	0	5	0	Spiro, H., Exs., of late ...	0	10	0
Bell, Mrs....	0	5	0	Merry, T. F., J.P. ...	0	10	0
Lewis, W., "Ellengowan"	0	5	0	McIntyre, J. S....	0	10	0
Clements, C., "Talgai" ...	0	5	0	Groom, W. H., M.L.A. ...	0	10	0
Sums under 5s., ditto	0	5	0	Ross and Hodgen	0	10	0
Sums under 5s.	0	7	6	Stevens and Co.	0	10	0
				Holberton, F. H.	0	10	0
STANTHORPE.				Ruthnung, H. L. E.... ...	0	10	0
Hardaker, B., J.P.,				Black, G. and J.	0	10	0
"Whealedith" Tin Mine	1	1	0	Garget, J., Mayor ...	0	10	0
Sullivan, D., ditto	0	3	0	Stevens, S. T.	0	10	0
Westhoven, Charles G.,				Cobb, J.	0	10	0
Brisbane Tin Mine ...	1	1	0	Blackburn, J.	0	8	6
A Friend. ditto	1	0	0	Woodhouse, G.	0	8	0
Allison, W., Sugar Loaf ...	0	10	0	Henderson, R. C.	0	5	0
Laird, R., ditto ...	0	10	0	Hodgson, I. L....	0	5	0
Howell, W., ditto ...	0	5	0	Collins, T....	0	5	0
Jenner, Mrs., Bookookoo-				Green, W. C.	0	5	0
rarra	0	5	0	Robertson, J. H.	0	5	0
Gillam, W. G., Gap Hotel	0	5	0	Groth, W.	0	5	0
				Morrison, A.	0	5	0
TOOWOOMBA.				Harris, Inspector of Police	0	5	0
Workmen on Southern and				Dakers, R. A.	0	5	0
Western Railway,Queens-				Hudson, H.	0	5	0
land, per Alfred Thomas,				Griffiths, G.	0	5	0
Esq.	33	4	0	Bennett, G. F....	0	5	0
Taylor, Hon. J., M.L.C. ...	2	2	0	Hooper, G.	0	5	0
Cruise, R., Westbrook Hall	2	2	0	Devine, W. R....	0	5	0
Cocks, C.	2	2	0	Keogh, P....	0	5	0
X.	1	1	0	Ruthning, J.	0	5	0
Cribb, B., P.M...	1	1	0	Harris, J.	0	5	0
Hamilton and Son	1	1	0	Wilcox, E...	0	5	0
Aland, R., J.P.	1	1	0	S. H....	0	5	0
Gregory,Hon.F.T.,M.L.C.,				Sums under 5s...	0	11	6
"Carlaxton"	1	1	0				
Beer, J. and W.	1	1	0	**WARWICK.**			
Campbell, J. C. and W....	1	1	0	Macansh, John D., J.P.,			
Robinson, E. W., J.P. ...	1	1	0	"Canning Downs" ...	5	0	0
Benjamin, D. and J.	0	10	6	Somerset, Fitzroy, P.M....	1	1	0
Proprietors of Darling				Horwitz and Co.	1	1	0
Downs *Gazette*	0	10	6	Hubert, H.	1	1	0
Abraham, Rev. T. ...	0	10	0	Slade, W. B., J.P., "Glen-			
Weale, Mrs.	0	10	0	gallan"...	1	1	0
Turner, Mrs.	0	10	0	Green, C. H., J.P., "Goom-			
Walker, C. E.	0	10	0	burra"	1	1	0
Hume, W. C.	0	10	0	Coutts, Bros., "North Toul-			
Boyce, J. A., C.P.S.... ...	0	10	0	burra"	1	1	0
Smith, J. Thornlow... ...	0	10	0	Margetts, Dr., J.P.	1	0	0
Mackenzie, J.P.	0	10	0	Taylor, Dr., J.P.	1	0	0
Stirling, J....	0	10	0	Evenden, S.	1	0	0
Wonderley, J., J.P.... ...	0	10	0				

	£	s.	d.
Tilley, T., J.P., "Chiverton"	1	0	0
McDougall, M. S., J.P., "Lindhurst"	1	0	0
Parkinson, Rev. M. H. ...	0	10	6
Veitch, J. A., "Glengallan"	0	10	6
Morgan, J., M.L.A.... ...	0	10	6
Dickson, W. M., "Stonehenge"	0	10	6
Cowton and Irwin	0	10	6
Dandie, Rev. Alex.... ...	0	10	6
Matthews, Rev. J.	0	10	0
Lethbridge, J. T.	0	10	0
Dunlop, J. H.	0	10	0
Wilkins, R.	0	10	0
Ross, J. R.	0	10	0
Benjamin and Co.	0	10	0
Aland, R.	0	10	0
Saunders, S.	0	10	0
South, C. J. W.	0	10	0
Dinte, H. D.	0	10	0
Kircher, J.	0	6	0
Jarrett, E.	0	5	0
Ryan, J.	0	5	0
Greiner, W.	0	5	0
Isambert, C. J.... ...	0	5	0
Barth, C.	0	5	0
Thompson, E. W.	0	5	0
Spreadborough, W.... ...	0	5	0
Spreadborough, F.	0	5	0
Clarke, D....	0	5	0
Prussong, T.	0	5	0
Giblett, H.	0	5	0
Gilm, C.	0	5	0
Railway Station Master ...	0	5	0
Voss, J. P., "Glengallan"	0	5	0

	£	s.	d.
Beeson, T.	£0	5	0
Johnson, T. A....	0	5	0
Hoffman, P.	0	5	0
Lavers, W.	0	5	0
Davis, Miss	0	5	0
Woodcock, C. A. J., J.P., C.P.S.	0	5	0
Canny, J. A.	0	5	0
Millar, Mrs.	0	5	0
Hurford and Co.	0	5	0
Chavasse, G. W.	0	5	0
Roggenkamp, C.	0	5	0
Sums under 5s.	1	6	6
Advertisements free in *Warwick Argus*			

YANDILLA STATION.

	£	s.	d.
Gore and Co.	2	2	0
Gore, F. A.	1	1	0
Gore, R. W.	1	1	0
Gore, G. R.	1	1	0
Kennard, S. B....	1	1	0
Carroll, J....	1	0	0
Watson, J.	1	0	0
Williams, E., J.P.	1	0	0
Shaw, T.	0	13	0
Fitzmaurice, G. R.	0	10	6
Hodgkinson, Dr.	0	10	6
Purcell, J. P.	0	10	6
Baillie, J.	0	10	0
Pont, J.	0	5	0
McDonald, J.	0	5	0
Savage, M...	0	5	0
Johnson, J...	0	5	0
Mara, J.	0	5	0
Bulling, H.	0	5	0
Dowling, P.	0	5	0
Lau, Professor	0	5	0

SCHOOL FEES, AND PAYMENTS FOR CLOTHING.

	£	s.	d.
Allison, Mrs.	19	10	9
Ditto, (Clothing)	2	9	0
Ditto, (Music)	2	2	0
Adams, T....	2	10	0
Barnes, T...	9	0	0
Ditto, (Clothing)... ...	1	10	0
Britcheno, Mr....	4	0	0
Bailey, — per Mrs. Duggan	5	0	0
Ditto, (Clothing) ...	2	6	6
Churchill, H.	3	15	0
Ditto, (Clothing) ...	3	17	10
Cameron, Mrs. (Ditto) ...	0	13	0
Dawson, Mrs.	10	0	0
Durham, Mr.	4	0	0
Ditto, (Clothing) ...	2	7	6
Darcey, Mr.	7	10	0
Ditto, (Clothing) ...	0	6	0
Everingham, Mr.	6	10	0
Ellis, T. (Clothing) ...	5	0	0
Farr, J.	15	0	0
Gilbert, Mr.	12	10	0
Golding, C. (Clothing) ...	5	1	8
Harrison, G. D.	10	0	0
Ditto, (Clothing) ...	1	11	6
Hurst, Rev. G...	62	10	0
Hall, W.	8	0	0
Hudson, Mr. ... ''' ...	15	0	0
Hill, J. (Clothing) ...	3	18	9
Haberling, G. (Ditto) ...	6	0	0
Jones, Mrs.	8	0	0
Jamison, Mrs. (Clothing)	5	0	0
Kluga, Mrs.	1	5	0
Milroy, Mrs.	5	0	0
Margan, Mrs. (Apprenticing)	10	0	0
McLaughlen, A. J.	25	10	0
Ditto, (Clothing) ...	6	6	6
McDonald, Brisbane ...	7	0	0
McDonald, — per Mr. S. Moore	15	0	0
Northcote, Mr....	3	0	0
Osmond, Mrs. (Clothing)	0	4	6
Prevost, Mrs.	2	10	0
Phelps, Mr., per W. P. Woolcott, Esq.	4	0	0
Queensland Government...	74	0	0
Reuter, Mr.	1	10	0
Ditto, (Clothing) ...	0	10	6
Rogan, E....	2	10	0
Ditto, Clothing	1	15	0
Smith, C. H.	20	0	0
Smith, S.	4	10	0
Selby, Mr. (Clothing) ...	10	0	0
Tasmanian Government...	74	0	0
Todd, Mrs. (Clothing) ...	1	5	0
Thomson, Mrs. (Ditto) ...	5	0	0
Tyrrell, Mr. (Ditto) ...	6	0	0
Wehrman, Mr., per W. Butler, (Clothing and School fees)	10	12	9
Willbow, G.	12	10	0
Ditto, (Clothing) ...	7	12	3
Wilshire, F. R.	11	0	0
Wearne, Mrs. (Clothing)	0	10	0

MISCELLANEOUS DONATIONS AND SERVICES.

Rendered during the year ending September 30th, from the following, and thankfully acknowledged : —

Barker, Mrs., Newtown, Toys, &c.

Barker, F. J., *Illustrated London News, Punch,* &c.

Baptist, John, Esq., Flowers at different times.

Colonial Sugar Works Company, Casks of Treacle.

Civil Service Musical Society, Free admission to Concerts for Blind Pupils.

Clarke, F. H., Esq., Free admission and treat for the Children to Wesleyan Industrial Exhibition, William Street.

Dickson, Mrs., Case of Oranges.

Davis, Mrs., Newtown, Wringing Machine.

Dangar, F. H., Esq., Christmas Treat.

Elsen, Mr. Brisbane, £1 to buy fruit for the Children.

Fache, Mrs., Cleveland House, Books for Library, Toys, &c., on two different occasions.

Fairfax, Mrs. C., Numbers of *Illustrated London News* and Music.

Gibson, — Esq., £2 to buy Treat and Toys for the Children.

Goodlet, Mrs., Prizes for Needlework.

Griffiths, Mrs., Ashfield, Quantity of passion fruit.

Gratuitous Copies of *Illustrated Sydney News, Australian Churchman,* and *Sydney Mail* from the Proprietors.

Hay, Mrs. Picnic to all pupils and officers, Buns, lollies, butter and eggs, at different times.

Holt, Mrs., "The Warren," Buns for Good Friday.

Haig, Mrs., Monthly Number of *Old Jonathan.*

Henry, Mrs. James, Dentistry.

Hill, Rev. Thomas, Case of Bananas.

Hurst, Mrs. G., Butter at different times.

Hungerford, Rev. S., Books for Library.

Harrison, G. D., Collection and assistance to the Collector in Brisbane.

Joy, E., Esq., Donation of £2 for Drawing Pupils.

Jeanneret, C. E., Esq., A free trip by steamer to Gladesville to pupils and friends.

Leeds, Mr., Orange, Case of Fresh Meat.

Love, Mrs., Parcels of lollies at different times.

Moore, Mr. S., Castle Hill, Cases of fruit.

Milson, Mr., Free passages for children and Officers to North Shore during Holidays.

Parcels of Lace Samples, &c., from Messrs. Ross and Morgan's Warehouse.

Phillips, Mrs. Henry, Treat to Children of Buns, Cakes, Lollies, &c.

Stenteford, Mrs., Newtown, Five shillings for little Blind Children.

Shaw, Sergeant, No. 1 Highlanders, A sheep.

Sydney United Omnibus Company, Omnibus free of charge to Circular Quay and back.

Seymour, Mr., Donation of fish at different times.

Spalding, Mr., Young trees and flowers.

Spencer, Mr., Pitt Street, Admission free to Museum.

Smith, Mrs., Kurrajong, Case of Oranges.

Taylor, Rev. R., Picnic to Parramatta with St. Stephen's School children.

Taylor, Mr., St. Paul's College, Case of Oranges.

Wigzell, Mr., attendance monthly to cut Children's hair.

List of Clothing made in the year 1876, 1877 :—

70 Pillow Cases	43 Aprons
52 Sheets	6 Pinafores
70 Towels	10 Pairs of Trousers
20 Mosquito Nets	26 Chemises
11 Table Cloths	18 Pairs of Drawers
27 Dresses	2 Bodicies
10 Shirts	10 Petticoats
4 Night Shirts	10 Bed Covers
14 Night Dresses	
2 Coats	405 Articles.
43 Aprons	

Information and Directions relative to the Admission of Children to the Institution.

1. Applications must be in writing addressed to the Secretary, sent before the child is brought to the Institution, and should contain as full information as possible, the necessary forms can be obtained of the Hon. Secretary.

2. Pupils are admissible from any part of the colony of New South Wales, and under certain conditions, from Queensland, Tasmania, and New Zealand.

3. No child deficient in intellect, subject to fits, or unable to wash and dress itself, can be considered a fit subject for admission.

4. Children from seven to twelve years of age are eligible for admission, but in no case shall the age be above 15 years.

5. No order will be given by the Committee for a child's admission until the medical certificate has been obtained.

6. Children on entering the Institution are required to have two complete suits of clothing, for school or week-day wear, to be of dark colour, and a better suit for Sunday, and be provided with clothing (see list) by their parents or friends during their residence, each child must be provided with a Box or Trunk in which to keep clean clothing for use. If £5 is remitted the Committee will purchase outfit on admission.

7. Any amounts remitted to the Secretary for the purchase of clothing will be expended under the direction of the Committee of Management.

8. The fees payable in ordinary cases for the board, education, &c., of children in the Institution are :—£25 per annum ; in special cases a lower scale of fees is adopted.

9. In the case of pauper children, a certificate of inability to pay any fee must be obtained from known individuals.

10. The fees are payable in advance, and date from the time of admission.

11. Children cannot be permitted to leave the Institution unless with the direct sanction and authority of the Committee.

12. In addition to the usual educational course the girls are taught household duties, and the boys out-door and other work.

13. The vacations are 5 weeks at Christmas, and 1 week at Mid-Winter, and it is essential that pupils should return to the Institution on the day fixed to commence duties after each vacation, and with their clothing clean and in proper order. See List.

14. The average term of Residence in the Institution is for Deaf and Dumb pupils 6 to 8 years, and for Blind pupils 3 to 5 years.

15. The Parents and Friends of children are admitted once a fortnight, on Thursdays, between the hours of 12 noon and 3 p.m.

16. The Children are permitted to visit their friends once a month, on special application being made to the Committee.

17. Money orders should be made payable to the Secretary or Treasurer at the Head Office, Post Office, George-street, Sydney.

18. It is requested all communications be addressed to the undersigned,

ELLIS ROBINSON, *Hon. Secretary,*
at the Institution, or 486, George-street, Sydney.

NEW SOUTH WALES
Institution for the Deaf and Dumb and the Blind.
NEWTOWN ROAD.

The following quantity of Clothing is required for each child, to be supplied on its entering the Institution, which it is anticipated will, with a few additions and repairs, last for twelve months :—

For Boys.

2 Suits for week-day wear
1 Suit for Sunday ditto
4 Shirts, day—white or crimean
2 Ditto night
6 Pairs Socks
2 Caps or Felt Hats
6 Collars
6 Handkerchiefs
2 Pairs Cotton Braces
2 Neckties
1 Hair and 1 Tooth Brush
1 Rack and 1 Fine Tooth Comb
2 Pairs Boots

For Small Boys.

3 Holland Pinafores may be supplied.

For Girls.

3 Dresses for week-day wear
1 Dress for Sunday ditto
2 Petticoats, general use
1 Petticoat, Sunday ditto
6 Pairs Stockings or Socks
2 Hats
6 Plain Linen Collars or Frills
6 Handkerchiefs
1 Warm Jacket
6 Pairs Drawers
2 Pairs Stays or Bodices
3 Chemises
3 Night Dresses
6 Pinafores or Aprons
1 Rack and 1 Fine Tooth Comb
1 Hair and 1 Tooth Brush
2 Pairs Boots.

Each child to be provided with a Box or Trunk in which to keep Clothing when clean for use. The Clothing in all cases must be Dark Coloured. The Girls' Dresses may be Print for Summer wear, and Alpaca, Wincey, or similar material for Winter wear.

Boys' suits should be of Dark Coloured washing Tweed or other similar material. (Drill suits are not to be worn ; if sent, parents must provide for having them washed.)

ELLIS ROBINSON,
March 31, 1873. *Honorary Secretary.*

SPECIAL INFORMATION.

"The object of this Institution is the educating, and maintenance whilst so doing, of Deaf and Dumb or Blind children, from the age of seven years; to enable them to earn their own living, make them useful members of society, and prevent them becoming, as they would in most cases, a burden upon public charity in after years."

The Institution is open to Subscribers and other Visitors daily—Saturdays, Sundays, and holidays excepted,—from 2 to 4 p.m.

The Parents and Friends of children are admitted once a fortnight, on Thursdays, between the hours of 12 noon and 3 p m.

The children are permitted to leave the Institution to visit their friends once a month, on special application being made to the Committee.

Forms and all particulars for the admission of pupils into the Institution, and copies of the Rules and Regulations, can be obtained of the Honorary Secretary.

Subscriptions and Donations will be thankfully received and acknowledged by the Treasurer, the Secretary, or at the Institution. Donations or Bequests of over £100 are placed to a Perpetual Subscribers' Fund.

The Meetings of Committee are held on the Second Monday in each month, at 4 o'clock p.m. The Ladies Visiting Committee meet at the Institution, on the last Friday in the month, at 3 o'clock in the Winter, and half-past 3 o'clock in the Summer months.

Donations of Meat, Vegetables, Fruit (Fresh and Preserved,) are thankfully received and acknowledged; also clothing and Materials for the same will be thankfully accepted.

The cost of passages to and from the Institution must be paid by the Friends of the pupils. The Committee having no Fund for this purpose.

All communications to be addressed to Ellis Robinson, Honorary Secretary, at the Institution or 486, George-street, Sydney.

Money orders should be made payable to the Secretary or Treasurer at the Head Office, Post Office, St. Martin's, Sydney.

It is highly necessary that the Parents or Friends of children notify to the Secretary any change of Residence in case of illness, or other cause requiring immediate communication.

No. _ _____

NEW SOUTH WALES

𝕴nstitution for the 𝕯eaf & 𝕯umb, & the 𝕭lind.

——o——

COPY OF FORM OF RECOMMENDATION FOR ADMISSION.

1. State Christian Name and Surname, Age, and Religion of the Child recommended for admission, and Native Place..	
2. State Christian Names and Surnames of the Father and Mother, also trade or calling, and present residence...................	
3. State circumstances of the case ; also as to the amount that the Parents or Friends are able and willing to contribute towards the maintenance and education of the Child, and what security can be offered that such payments will be duly made......................	

Signature of two Subscribers to the Institution.......... { 1 _____
2 _____

Signature of Clergyman or Magistrate of the District in which the Child resides...... { 3 _____

Dated this _____ *day of* _____ 187

————o————   *No.* ____

DEAF AND DUMB CHILDREN.

————♦————

1. Name and Sex   ...   .

2. Age and date of Birth...   ...   .

3. Religion of Parents   ...   .

4. Native place...   ...   .

5. Usual Residence ...   .

6. Been afflicted from birth   ...   .

7. Affliction hereditary ; i.e., by direct
   transmission from the Parents ?   ...

8. Are any other members of the family
   or relatives of the Parents similarly
   afflicted ?   ...   .

9. Is the affliction single or double ?   ...

10. Has the single or double affliction
    always been present?...   ...   .

11. Is the power to hear sounds entirely
    absent ?   ...   .

12. Is the power to utter articulate sounds
    entirely absent ? ...   .

13. Has Child suffered from fright, grief,
    or other emotional causes ?   ...   ...

14. Has Child suffered from fits of any
    kind, fever, palsy, or injury to head
    or spine ?   ...   .

15. Has Child had Measles, Whooping
    Cough, or Scarlet Fever, and been
    vaccinated ? ...   .

16. Are the Parents in any degree related,
    if so, what is their consanguinity ?   ...

17. Does the Mother attribute the affliction
    to any circumstance occuring during
    her pregnancy ? ...   .

18. State condition of intellect ?   ...   ...

19. Is there any malformation of the in-
    terior of the mouth and throat ?   ...

20. State any peculiarities of stature, bodily
    configuration, &c...   ...   .

21. Are the Parents intemperate and
    profligate   ...   .

22. Are any other children similarly
    afflicted known to the Parents as
    resident in their neighbourhood ?   ...

23. How many other Children are there
    in family besides the Candidate ?   ...

24. Are both Parents alive ?   ...   .

Date of Admission.......................... Date of Leaving..........................

HISTORICAL STATEMENT of Candidate for Admission.

—o—

BLIND CHILDREN.   No._____

—o—

1. Name and Sex of Candidate? ... ... _____
2. Age and date of birthday? ... ... _____
3. Religion of Parents? ... ... _____
4. Native place? ... ... _____
5. Present Residence? ... ... _____
6. Been afflicted from birth if not at what age? ... ... _____
7. Affliction hereditary; i.e., by direct transmission from Parents? ... ... _____
8. Are any other members or relatives of the family similarly afflicted? ... ... _____
9. Is there any other defect of the senses? _____
10. Sight entirely Gone? ... ... _____
11. If from accident or disease, describe the circumstances connected with the origin of the Blindness? ... ... _____
12. Has any Surgical Operation been performed for the relief of the Blindness? _____
13. Has child suffered from fright, grief, or other emotional causes? ... ... _____
14. Has child suffered from fits of any kind, fever, palsy, or any injury to the head, face, or spine? ... ... _____
15. Has child had Measles, Whooping Cough, or Scarlet Fever, and been Vaccinated? ... ... _____
16. Are the Parents in any degree Related, what is their Consanguinity? ... ... _____
17. Does the Mother attribute the affliction, to any circumstance occuring during her Pregnancy? ... ... _____
18. State condition of intellect? ... ... _____
19. Any malformation of interior of mouth or throat? ... ... _____
20. State any peculiarities of Stature, Bodily Configuration, &c. ... ... _____
21. Are the Parents intemperate or profligate ... ... _____
22. Are any other children similarly afflicted, known to the Parents as resident in the neighbourhood? ... _____
23. How many other children are there in the family? ... ... _____
24. Are both Parents alive? ... ... _____

Date of Admission........................ Date of Leaving........................

MEDICAL CERTIFICATE.

I certify that I have this day examined..and have found............in good bodily health, and free from cutaneous and contagious disorders. I consider............a fit subject for admission to the Institution. Date........................18......

....*Honorary Medical Officer.*

FORM OF A BEQUEST

TO THE

New South Wales Institution for the Deaf, and Dumb, and the Blind.

I give and bequeath unto A. B. (or unto my said Executors—or my said Trustees as the case may be) the sum of .... upon trust to pay out of my Personal Estate to the Treasurer for the time being of "The New South Wales Institution for the Deaf and Dumb, and the Blind" such sum as a donation to the said Institution.

The following is the proper attestation to a Will :—

(*Signatures and Addresses.*)

Signed by the above-named testator as and for his last Will in our presence who in his presence at his request and in the presence of each other have sub-scribed our names as witnesses.

All Legacies and Donations of £50 and upwards are now placed to credit of a Perpetual Subscribers Fund as an Endowment.

TABULAR STATEMENT OF NAMES &c., of CHILDREN who have been Pupils of the Institution

from the Foundation 1860, until September, 1877.

DEAF AND DUMB CHILDREN.

No.	Name.	Age on Admission.	Religion.	Where Received from.	Date of Admission.	Date of Leaving.	Other Children in family.	Remarks.
1	Lorsey, Patrick	...	Roman Catholic	Sydney, N.S.W.	...	...		Apprentice to a Shoemaker.
2	Thorp, Joseph	14	Ditto	Ditto	...	...		Died.
3	Hagen, Felix	14	Ditto	Ditto	...	1860		Taken to Benevolent Asylum.—Idiotic.
4	Patterson, Henry	...	Protestant	Shoalhaven	...	...		Only a short time a pupil.
5	Lentz, Anne	...	Ditto	Sydney	...	...		Returned to friends.
6	Hurst, Susan	14	Ditto	Ditto	1860	...1862		Gone to a trade.
7	Poullon, William	...	Ditto	Ditto	...	...		Went to Scotland.
8	Carmichael, Edward	11	Roman Catholic	Ditto	1860	...		Gone to a trade.
9	Bridgement, Annie	4	Protestant	Ditto	1860	Feb. 1864		Since died.
10	Plowright, Selina	12	Ditto	Ditto	1860	Sept. 1863		
11	Pearson, Elizabeth	17	Ditto	Ditto	1860	June 1864		
12	Morrow, William	9	Ditto	Camperdown	1860 Jan.	1864		Gone to a trade—Bootmaker.
13	Logan, Thomas	10	Ditto	Sydney	1863 May	1866		
14	Murray, Richard	5	Roman Catholic	Ditto	1863 Aug.	1864		Gone to a trade—Engineer.
15	Mailley, Harriet	14	Protestant	Ditto	1862 Jan.	1864		
16	Keene, Lizzie	12	Roman Catholic	Ditto	1860	1867		
17	Lynch, Deborah	8	Protestant	Ditto	1860	1864		Went to Brisbane.
18	Gleadhill, Mary Jane	14	Ditto	Picton	1863 April	1861		Returned to her friends.
19	Hill, Emma	9	Ditto	Sydney	1860	1866		Living with friends in Victoria.
20	Mailley, Richard	13	Ditto	Ditto	1865 Jan.	1866		In service now.
21	Smith, Thomas	14	Ditto	Hinton, Hunter River	1860	1864		Gone to a trade—Bootmaker.
22	McLaughlin, Richard	15	Ditto	Warialda, N.S.W.	1862 Feb.	May 1864	...	Labourer.
23	McLaughlin, Thomas	12	Ditto	Warialda, N.S.W.	1862 "	1864	...	Returned to his friends.
24	Lewis, William	13	Ditto	Pyrmont, Sydney	1862 Oct.	Dec. 1865	...	Returned to his friends.
25	Hart, Elizabeth	16	Ditto	New Zealand	1862 Feb.	Mar. 1866	...	Absconded and since dead.
26	Bates, Kate	11	Roman Catholic	Sofala, N.S.W.	1861 Dec.	Dec. 1865	...	Returned to New Zealand.
27	Kelly, Eleanor	11	Ditto	Appin	1861 April	June 1869	9	Returned to her friends.
28	Wright, Christiana J.	11	Ditto	Sydney	1862 Feb.	Sep. 1865	...	Ditto ditto.
29	Thompson, Jane	7	Unitarian	Parramatta	1862 "	Oct. 1865	...	Ditto ditto.
30	Egglestone, William	5	Protestant	Shellharbour	1862 Aug.	1873	4	Ditto ditto.
31	Richardson, William	11	Ditto	Richmond	1862 Jan.	June 1875	4	Ditto ditto. Farm Servant.
32	Waterson, Rebecca	10	Ditto	Concord	1864 Nov.	Mar. 186?		Went to a trade—Saddler.

Note (spanning the "Other Children in family" column for the upper rows): Most of these Children were received into the Institution on opening. From the length of time elapsed it is difficult to obtain information about them.

No.	Name	Age	Religion	Where from	Adm. Month	Adm. Year	Disch. Month	Disch. Year	No.	Remarks
33	Thompson, Mary Ann	10	Ditto	Fitzroy Iron Mines	Feb.	1865	Feb.	1872	1	Sent to Newcastle Institution for Imbeciles.
34	Golding, Mary Jane	10	Ditto	Irish Town, N.S.W.	May.	1865		1873	4	Now in the Institution.
35	Farmer, William	11	Ditto	Newcastle, ditto	Nov.	1865			8	Gone to work at a Coal Mine.
36	McKenzie, Catherine	13	Ditto	Wentworth, ditto	July	1865	Nov.	1868	6	Returned to friends. Dressmaker.
37	Morrison, William	16	Ditto	Nerigunda, ditto	July	1865	Dec.	1868		,,
38	Milner, Alfred Herbert	13	Ditto	Broadwater, Nanoi R.	Dec.	1865	Jan.	1870		,,
39	Sullivan, Catherine	6	Roman Catholic	Bathurst, N.S.W.	Jan.	1866	Feb.		6	Now in the Institution—Teacher.
40	Cameron, Christina	13	Protestant	Goulburn, ditto	Feb.	1866	May	1869		Returned to her friends.
41	Stewart, Mary Anne	5	Ditto	Lachlan, ditto	May	1866			4	Now in the Institution.
42	Eggleston, Mary Anne	5	Ditto	Shellharbour, ditto	Aug.	1866			1	
43	Wearne, Anne Susan	15	Ditto	Newcastle, ditto	Sept.	1866	Sept.	1871	9	Returned to her friends.
44	Singer, Louisa Sophia	12	Ditto	Hobart Town, Tasmania	Nov.	1866	Nov.	1871	5	Gone to a trade—Shoemaker.
45	Love, Thomas	8	Ditto	Rockhampton, Queensld.	July	1867			3	Ditto ditto—Tinsmith.
46	Smart, Albert	18	Ditto	Sydney, N.S.W.	Aug.	1867	Aug.	1875		Left the Institution.
47	Ryder, Henrietta	10	Ditto	Windsor, N.S.W.	Sept.	1867			5	Returned to friends.
48	Pollock, Alexander	12	Ditto	King's Plains, Queensld.	Nov.	1868	Nov.	1875	8	Returned to parents.
49	Saber, Barnard	13	Hebrew	Sydney	April	1868			3	Taken away by his friends.
50	Walsh, Thomas	11	Roman Catholic	Ditto	Jan.	1868			3	Returned to Brisbane.
51	Murphy, John	6	Ditto	Ipswich, Queensland	Feb.	1869			4	Now in the Institution.
52	Jamison, Archibald	6	Protestant	Ditto, ditto	April	1869			4	Returned to parents.
53	Hurst, Edwin	6	Ditto	Sydney	,,	1869	Feb.	1877	4	Now in the Institution.
54	Jordon, Daniel William	4	Protestant	Queanbeyan	April	1869			4	Left ,, the Institution.
55	Jordon, Charles		Ditto	Ditto	,,	1869			5	Gone to a trade—Dressmaker.
56	Byrnes, William	8	Roman Catholic	New England, N.S.W.	May	1869	Dec.	1876	1	Ditto ditto.
57	Smails, Susan	9	Protestant	Manning River	July	1869	June	1877		Idiotic & removed to Asylum for Insane.
58	Coles, Mary Isabel	7	Ditto	Sydney	Nov.	1866	Dec.	1866	7	Returned to New Zealand.
59	Smithers, Thomas	9	Ditto	Araluen	May	1869	Feb.	1877	4	Now in the Institution.
60	Selby, John	5	Ditto	Auckland, New Zealand	Oct.	1869			10	Returned to friends.
61	Farr, Arthur Thomas	10	Ditto	Redfern, N.S.W.	,,	1869	Dec.	1875	3	Returned to her friends to Victoria.
62	Sparke, Maria Goldfinch	11	Ditto	West Maitland, N.S.W.	June	1870	May	1871	6	
63	Boulton, Adelaide Rosina	9	Ditto	McLeay River, N.S.W.	Aug.	1870			2	Now in the Institution.
64	Jessup, Emmeline	5	Ditto	Ryde, Parramatta River	Sep.	1870			7	Returned to friends.
65	Chapman, Bridget	10	Ditto	Sydney	Oct.	1870			1	
66	Churchill, Emma Deborah	10	Ditto	Port McQuarie	Aug.	1870	Dec.	1875	2	
67	Howe, Frederick	7	Ditto	Newtown, N.S.W.	Sep.	1870	Nov.	1870	1	A Saddler.
68	Carpenter, John Thomas	12	Ditto	Ryde, Parramatta River	Oct.	1870			2	Idiotic and returned to his friends.
69	McDonald, Augustus John	7	Ditto	Concord, ditto	Jan.	1871			1	Now in the Institution.
70	Bridgement, Anna Elizab.	6	Ditto	Sydney	Feb.	1871	July	1871	4	Returned to her friends.
71	Britcheno, Halston Elizab.	5	Ditto	Waterloo, N.S.W.	Mar.	1871			1	Now in the Institution.
72	Hurst, Herbert	11	Ditto	Wollongong	July	1871	Aug.	1877	4	Returned to Parents.
73	Durham, John Edwin		Ditto	Singleton, N.S.W.	Jan.	1872			4	Now in the Institution.
74	D'Arey, William		Roman Catholic	Sydney	Feb.	1872			2	
75	Arell, Henry	11	Protestant	Brisbane, Queensland	Mar.	1872	Dec.	1876	6	Draughtsman Works Dep. Queensland Gov.

TABULAR STATEMENT OF NAMES, &c.—Continued.

DEAF AND DUMB CHILDREN.—Continued.

No.	Name.	Age on Admission.	Religion.	Where Received from.	Date of Admission.	Date of Leaving.	Other Children in family.	Remarks.
76	Smith, Henry Caulfield	9	Protestant	Newtown	Mar. 1872	...	6	Now in the Institution.
77	Jordan, Eliza Jane	6	Ditto	Quemberan	April 1872	Dec. 1873	5	Idiotic—taken to Newcastle Asylum.
78	McLaughlen, Frank	12	Ditto	Goorah, N.S.W.	1872	...	7	Now in the Institution.
79	Cameron, Lachlan	9	Ditto	Goulburn	May 1872	...	6	Now in the Institution.
80	Rodgers, Ellen	9	Roman Catholic	Coolac, N.S.W.	Sept. 1872	Dec. 1876	6	Returned to parents.
81	Goldsworthy, James	8	Protestant	Adelaide, S.A.	1872	...	0	Returned to his friends.
82	Harriss, Laura Eva	9	Ditto	Wollombi, N.S.W.	1872	1875	4	Returned to her friends.
83	White, Ida	5	Ditto	Merriwa, ditto	1872	...	1	Died.
84	Wehrman, Adolph	9	Protestant	Ipswich, Queensland	1872	...	1	Now in the Institution.
85	Ruwald, Elizabeth Mary	10	Roman Catholic	Newcastle, N.S.W.	Feb. 1873	...	5	Returned to her friends.
86	Jones, Martha	8	Protestant	Clarence Town, ditto	1873	...	4	Now in the Institution.
87	Jones, Annie	6	Ditto	Ditto ditto, ditto	1873	...	4	,, ,,
88	Smith, Margaret	18	Ditto	South Creek, ditto	1873	...	1	,, ,,
89	King, Margaret	9	Roman Catholic	Queensland	Aug. 1873	...	0	,, ,,
90	Ryan, Mary Anne	13	Ditto	Hobart Town, Tasmania	1873	...	2	Returned to Tasmania.
91	Ransley, Clara	12	Protestant	Moruya, N.S.W.	June 1874	Nov. 1876	10	Now in the Institution.
92	Fitzpatrick, James	6	Roman Catholic	Moonby, "	Aug. 1874	...	3	,, ,,
93	Wilbow, George	11	Protestant	Armidale	1874	...	3	,, ,,
94	Tyrrell, William	7½	Ditto	Ditto	Jan. 1875	...	5	,, ,,
95	Tyrrell, Joseph	4½	Ditto	Brisbane, Queensland	1875	...	5	,, ,,
96	Harrison, Herbert Cornish	7	Protestant	Ditto	Jan. 1875	...	3	,, ,,
97	Harrison, William Smith	6	Ditto	Ditto	1875	...	3	,, ,,
98	Barnes, Eliza	5	Ditto	Moonbi, N.S.W.	1875	...	3	,, ,,
99	Bailey, Eliza Jane	10	Ditto	Fish River, Bathurst	Feb. 1875	...	7	,, ,,
100	Osman, William Edward	7	Roman Catholic	Sydney	Mar. 1875	...	5	,, ,,
101	Haberling, Albert	12	Protestant	Rockhampton, Q.	April 1875	...	2	,, ,,
102	Jordan, Richard Mehegan	6	Ditto	Queanbeyan	April 1875	...	2	Has 2 Brothers inmates.
103	Northcote, Margaret Ann	7	Ditto	Brisbane	June 1875	...	6	Now in the Institution.
104	Cox, Thomas	10	Roman Catholic	Sydney	June 1875	Dec. 1876	3	Returned to parents.
105	King, Anne	7	Ditto	Queensland	July 1875	...	5	Has a Sister an inmate.
106	Reuter, C.	6	Protestant	Grafton	June 1875	...	7	Now in the Institution.
107	Dawson, Burt	12	Ditto	Denison Town, N.S.W.	Dec. 1876	...	4	Incapable of receiving Instruction.
108	McGillivray, Jane	14	Ditto	Kiama	Feb. 1876	Mar. 1876	3	Now in the Institution.
109	Prevost, Alice Maud	7	Ditto	Newcastle	Feb. 1876	...	5	Now in the Institution.
110	Pickard, Maria	7	Ditto	St. Leonards	Mar. 1876	April 1876	6	Idiotic. Returned to friends.

No.	Name	Age	Religion	Place	Admitted	Year	Left	Year	No.	Now in the Institution.
111	Begent, Laura Alice...	7	Protestant ...	Sydney... ...	June	1876	...	...	3	Now in the Institution.
112	McDonald, Robert ...	12	Ditto ...	Brisbane ...	May	1876	...	...	5	,,
113	Phelps, Catherine M.	12	Roman Catholic	Sydney... ...	Aug.	1876	...	...	4	,,
114	Thompson, Thomas...	12	Protestant ...	Rockhampton ...	Jan.	1877	...	...	3	,,
115	Hall, Albert ...	9	Ditto ...	Manning River ...	,,	,,	...	...	4	,,
116	Griffiths, Mary A. ...	10	Ditto ...	Tamworth ...	,,	,,	...	...	5	,,
117	Wilshire, L. K. ...	9	Ditto ...	Berrima ...	Feb.	,,	...	...	6	,,
118	Ritchie, Jane ...	7	Ditto ...	Ipswich ...	July	,,	...	...	5	,,
119	Glode, August ...	11	Ditto ...	Queensland...	,,	,,	...	...	4	,,
120	Adams, Thomas ...	7	Ditto ...	Maneroo ...	,,	,,	...	...	4	,,

BLIND CHILDREN.

No.	Name	Age	Religion	Place	Admitted	Year	Left	Year	No.	Remarks
1	Adams, Edmund ...	13	Protestant ...	Newtown ...	Mar.	1869	Dec.	1870	11	Returned to his friends.
2	Worsley, Sarah Ann	10	Ditto ...	Camperdown ...	,,	1869	Mar.	1874	3	,, ,, her
3	Saunders, John W. ...	8	Ditto ...	Icely Copper Mines	,,	1869	...	...	1	Now in the Institution. Chair caner.
4	Winmill, James A. ...	13	Ditto ...	Sydney, N.S.W. ...	Aug.	1869	Jan.	1870	3	Left the Colony.
5	Driscoll, John B. ...	5	Ditto ...	Rockhampton ...	Sept.	1869	,,	1874	3	Gone to a Trade.
6	McQuade, Susan Teresa	10	Roman Catholic	Sydney... ...	Nov.	1869	...	...	2	Now in the Institution.
7	Ellis, John Frank ...	8	Protestant ...	Singleton, N.S.W. ...	Jan.	1870	Dec.	1876	3	Cancer. Returned to parents.
8	Allison, George Robert	5	Ditto ...	Brisbane, Queensland	May	1871	July	1877	2	Returned to parents.
9	Todd, Mary Jane ...	6	Ditto ...	Rockhampton ...	Jan.	1871	...	...	0	Now in the Institution.
10	Kluga, Mary Anne ...	6	Roman Catholic	Grenfel, N.S.W. ...	June	1871	...	...	2	,, ,,
11	Hicks, Mary Ann ...	10	Protestant ...	Bowen, Queensland ...	Sept.	1872	...	...	1	,, ,,
12	Smith, Anne ...	9	Ditto ...	Braidwood ...	,,	1872	...	...	4	,, ,,
13	Grube, John ...	12	Ditto ...	Sydney... ...	July	1873	Jan.	1874	4	,, ,,
14	Everingham, Henrietta	12	Ditto ...	Windsor, N.S.W. ...	,,	1873	June	1877	7	Returned to parents.
15	Read, Sophia Jane ...	9	Ditto ...	Sydney... ...	Jan.	1874	...	...	1	Now in the Institution.
16	Mercer, Thomas ...	9½	Ditto ...	Tasmania... ...	July	1874	...	...	0	,, ,,
17	Pike, James Henry ...	12	Ditto ...	Newcastle ...	April	1875	...	...	4	,, ,,
18	Hill, Bell Leonard ...	12	Ditto ...	Cobboro ...	Feb.	1876	...	...	6	,, ,,
19	Milroy, Matthew ...	10	Ditto ...	Newtown ...	April	1876	...	...	6	,, ,,
20	Hudson, Louisa E. ...	12	Ditto ...	Paddington ...	Aug.	1876	...	...	6	,, ,,
21	Gilbert, David ...	16	Ditto ...	Newcastle ...	Feb.	1877	...	...	7	,, ,,
22	Usherwood, Alice ...	8	Ditto ...	Tasmania ...	,,	,,	...	...	8	,, ,,
23	Rogan, James ...	12	Roman Catholic	Parkes ...	April	,,	...	...	4	,, ,,
24	Townsend, William...	12	Protestant ...	Brisbane ...	July	,,	...	...	0	,, ,,

NOTE.—A reference to the tables will show that 144 Children, 120 Deaf and Dumb, and 24 Blind, have been received. Of these 74 have left to return to their friends and homes. 6 were found to be Idiotic, and beyond the influence of education, and were removed to Asylums for Insane, one died. 70 now remain. In 15 of the families are two or more deaf and dumb. 115 of the children belong to New South Wales, 21 from Queensland, 2 New Zealand, 6 Tasmania, and South Australia.

The receipt of a copy of the Reports of each of the undermentioned Institutions is thankfully acknowledged :—

Ulster Society for the Deaf and Dumb and Blind.
London Association for Promoting Welfare of the Blind.
Liverpool School for Indigent Blind.
Glasgow Asylum for Blind.
British Asylum for Deaf and Dumb Females, London.
Edinburgh Institution for Deaf and Dumb.
Victorian Institution for Deaf and Dumb.
Victorian Institution for the Blind.
New York Institution for Deaf and Dumb.
New York Institution for the Blind.
Proceedings Second Convention of American Instructors of the Blind.
New York State Institution for the Blind, Trustees and Officers Report.
Arkansas Institute for the Education of the Blind, U. S.
Illinois Institution for the Blind, U. S.
Pensylvania Working Home for Blind, U. S.
Missouri Institution for the Blind Men, U. S.
Report American Printing House for the Blind, U. S.
Minncsota Institution for Deaf and Dumb and Blind, U. S.
Kentucky Asylum for the Blind, U. S.
Georgia Academy for the Blind, U. S.
Bristol Asylum and School of Industry for the Blind.
California Institution for Deaf and Dumb and the Blind.
Maryland Institution for the Blind, Baltimore, U. S.

A Prayer for the Deaf and Dumb.

Lord God Almighty! merciful and holy,
　　At Thy feet we bend ;
We pray Thee for a little band and lowly :
　　O God attend.

Merciful Father! for Thy silent children
　　We would now plead ;
Oh! look upon them with Thy pitying favour,
　　See their need.

'Twas Thou that placed the spirit mute and passive
　　In its silent home ;
And made them, for a cause we dare not question,
　　Deaf and Dumb.

But though in silence lone condemned to wander
　　While here below ;
'Tis not Thy will that one of them should perish,
　　O! Father, no.

Lord God Almighty! merciful and gracious,
　　In His name we plead,
Who once " Ephphatha " breathed with sighs of pity
　　For their need.

Fain would we bring these children sad and silent
　　To His feet,
That they may catch His look of love and learn
　　His message sweet.

Help us then, gracious Lord, these lambs to gather
　　Thy fold within ;
Teach us how best their darkened minds to open—
　　Their souls to win.

And grant that as we strive to guide their footsteps
　　In the narrow road,
Our own from Thee may ne'er be found to wander,
　　Oh our God.

　　　　　　　　　　　　　　　　W. T.

MANUAL ALPHABET.

Double Hand.

A a	B b	C c	D d	E e
F f	G g	H h	I i	J j
K k	L l	M m	N n	O o
P p	Q q	R r	S s	T t
U u	V v	W w	X x	Y y
Z z	Good	Bad	& &	Equal

CLEMENT